February 2000

To David and Leah-

I hope this book is an encouragement to you in a small way as a repayment for the love and encouragement you have given to me.

God bless you both-

Amy

Walter Scott

Walter Scott

A Nineteenth-Century Evangelical

Mark G. Toulouse, Editor

St. Louis, Missouri

Cover: Ed Koehler
Interior design: Elizabeth Wright

This book is printed on acid-free, recycled paper.

Visit Chalice Press on the World Wide Web at
www.chalicepress.com

10 9 8 7 6 5 4 3 2 1 99 00 01 02 03

Library of Congress Cataloging–in–Publication Data

Toulouse, Mark G.
Walter Scott : A Nineteenth-Century Evangelical / Edited by Mark G. Toulouse.
p. cm.
ISBN 0-8272-4238-7
1. Scott, Walter, 1796–1861. 2. Restoration movement (Christianity). I. Scott, Walter, 1796–1861. II. Toulouse, Mark G., 1952–.
BX7343.S3W35 1999
286.6'092—dc21 98-50821
[B] CIP

Printed in the United States of America

Table of Contents

List of Contributors

Amy Collier Artman is a student in the Ph.D. program in History of Christianity at the University of Chicago Divinity School, Chicago, Illinois.

T. Dwight Bozeman is Professor of American Religious History in the School of Religion and the Department of History at the University of Iowa, Iowa City, Iowa.

Fred B. Craddock is Bandy Distinguished Professor of New Testament and Preaching Emeritus at Candler School of Theology, Emory University, Atlanta, Georgia.

James O. Duke is Professor of History of Christianity and History of Christian Thought at Brite Divinity School, Texas Christian University, Fort Worth, Texas.

David Edwin Harrell, Jr., is Daniel F. Breeden Eminent Scholar in the Humanities at Auburn University, Auburn, Alabama.

Peter M. Morgan is President of the Disciples of Christ Historical Society in Nashville, Tennessee.

Thomas H. Olbricht is Distinguished Professor Emeritus of Religion at Pepperdine University, Malibu, California. In retirement, he lives in South Berwick, Maine.

Mark G. Toulouse is Professor of American Religious History and Associate Dean at Brite Divinity School, Texas Christian University, Fort Worth, Texas.

D. Newell Williams is William G. Irwin Professor of Church History at Christian Theological Seminary, Indianapolis, Indiana.

Acknowledgments

This volume is a collaborative enterprise between the Disciples of Christ Historical Society and Brite Divinity School. It did not begin that way. In 1996–1997, the Disciples of Christ Historical Society and Brite Divinity School separately offered commemorative activities to celebrate the bicentennial of the birth of Walter Scott. The Historical Society sponsored three Kirkpatrick Lectures delivered by D. Newell Williams, Dean of Christian Theological Seminary. Williams lectured at the Pennsylvania and West Virginia regional assemblies of the Christian Church (Disciples of Christ), and also before the representatives of the three branches of the Stone-Campbell Movement at the trustees meeting of the Historical Society in the fall of 1996. Peter Morgan, president of the Historical Society, was also "on the road" bringing about one dozen lectures on Scott based upon the Philip Fall Lecture he gave in September 1996 at the First Christian Church, Frankfort, Kentucky, and upon the Ruth and Edward Boden Lectures he delivered at Palm Lake Christian Church in St. Petersburg, Florida.

Meanwhile, Brite Divinity School hosted a series of lectures on Scott as part of its celebration of the bicentennial of his birth. Lecturers included David E. Harrell, Amy Artman, James O. Duke, and T. Dwight Bozeman. Fred Craddock preached at the event as his way of honoring the memory of Walter Scott. This joint venture began with the attendance of Society archivist David McWhirter at the Brite lectures. The material of these separate celebrations was deemed of such quality as to merit life in a more lasting form, namely a book. The Society and the Divinity School have been in dialogue about issues related to its publication. Both have provided significant financial support for the project. In addition, Mark G. Toulouse, coordinator of the Brite lecture series and Professor of American Religious History at the Divinity School, has edited the work and has assisted in fund-raising. The Historical Society has provided leadership in publication and subvention issues. This partnership between Brite and the Historical Society has been particularly enjoyable. It is the hope of these parties that those who read this book will find the experience equally gratifying.

Sizable financial support for this project has been received from both Brite Divinity School and the Historical Society. In the case of the former, Dean Leo Perdue graciously found funds to support both the original symposium on Scott and the publication of this volume. In the case of the latter, the Disciples of Christ Historical Society has lent strong financial support through the James M. and Mary Dudley Seale Publications Fund. Other contributions to this project have come from a few individuals and congregations who have lent special support for this project. Jack and Laura Riehl of Bellevue, Washington, made a generous contribution toward this volume. Both have a strong interest in the history of the Stone-Campbell-Scott movement and have been active teachers and workers among Churches of Christ. This volume was also partially funded in memory of Ruth and Edward Boden by family and friends of Palm Lake Christian Church, St. Petersburg, Florida. The Bodens and Riehls, like Walter Scott before them, have served the ministry of local Christian churches with the fullness of all the gifts and talents with which God has blessed them.

Mark G. Toulouse
Peter M. Morgan

FOREWORD

Walter Scott: The Artistry of His Ministry

Peter M. Morgan

Walter Scott, as a young man, played the flute. This book celebrates his life for many more accomplishments but I wish to speak of Walter Scott the flute player. More than any other of our founders, Walter Scott was an artist. The purpose of this essay is to discuss knowledge, an appropriate and agreeable topic to Scott, as Americans moved beyond the so-called Age of Reason or Enlightenment. His life teaches about knowing because he was a preacher-educator with the heart of an artist.

Learning, as Americans have been taught, is a matter of detachment, distance, division and analysis, objectivity, skepticism, verification of unarguable fact. René Descartes propelled us in that direction with his famous "I think, therefore I am." Every reality is to be doubted. But, finally, the one thing he could not doubt was that he must exist because he found himself engaged in a process of thinking. Doubt everything. Truth is only verifiable objective fact in this hermeneutic of suspicion. Reason alone will be the sunshine which melts the cloud of superstition.

Disciples arose from this rationalistic tradition. To believe is simple. You simply read or hear the self-evidently clear information of the New Testament and you will believe. Belief is a simple consequence of getting the facts and getting them straight. There is even ridicule of those who don't "get it." If you are so dull as to read the facts of the New Testament and still not believe, then you must enter the kingdom, if at all, by the fool's gate. Walter Scott stands squarely in that tradition. Yet, in ways he himself may not have fully comprehended, he transcended that concept of how we learn and know. He is a good starting guide to move us beyond a purely rationalistic understanding of knowledge. Read Scott on the importance of art and education:

> Divest education of study in the arts, and you divest it of a chief element. If you break not the shaft, if you raze not the foundation, you at least strike from the elevation to which it is entitled the chief ornament of the column of education; you dethrone its capital and negative the fairest forms and loveliest specimens of human genius to which society has given birth in every age of the world, from him who, before the flood, invented the organ, down to Handel, Haydn, and Mozart; ...from him who sculptured out for everlasting admiration, the Venus de Medicis, and horrific Laocoön, down to David; from him whose pencil breathed life upon the walls of Grecian temples, down to Raphael the sublime, and Michelangelo...[1]

Knowing is more than fact-finding. Walter Brueggemann, in his Lyman Beecher lectures at Yale, returned to his listeners a simple phrase from Walt Whitman, "Finally comes the poet."[2] Brueggemann used the phrase to proclaim that Americans have falsely ascribed power to the advertisers, the generals, the politicians, the moguls of the entertainment industry. Those who have real power to influence our destiny are the playwrights, the storytellers, and the poets. I borrow the Brueggemann/Whitman phrase in order to raise a question about the meaning of knowledge. Walter Scott is both illustration and witness to my belief that human beings only fully know when they possess the heart of an artist.

---

[1]William Baxter, *Life of Walter Scott* (Cincinnati: Bosworth, Chase & Hall, 1874), p. 367.

[2]Walter Brueggemann, *Finally Comes the Poet: Daring Speech for Proclamation* (Minneapolis: Fortress Press, 1989), p. 6.

Music can be notes printed on a page. Music can be complex theories of composition. Music can be the history of the development of the art, from the sustained grunts of primitive people down to the latest rock and roll hit (sometimes it sounds like there is not much difference between the two). But for music to be music, it must transcend analysis and communication of fact. Music must be played, listened to, heard in a way to connect deeply with something in the human spirit that probably transcends language. Music is known only fully, for example, when a Beethoven sonata surrounds and intimately engages the listener. Music is carried on the pulses of rhythm: sound/silence; engagement/rest. Learning also has a rhythm: engagement/rest/reflection; sound/silence/appropriation. Walter Scott knew what music and learning had in common. He especially appreciated the way music could move the human spirit. A wonderful story told by his brother James illustrates this point.

In early nineteenth century Scotland, many people enjoyed a playful New Year's custom known as "first foot." Each person tried to be the "first foot" to cross the threshold of the homes of special friends after midnight of New Year's Eve. The first foot brought good luck for the coming year to the inhabitants of the house. As a part of the festivities nearing midnight on New Year's Eve, the citizens of Edinburgh playfully made their way through the streets to the homes of their friends. While he was a student, Walter Scott and his brother James were among them.

On one particular New Year's Eve, James could not find his brother Walter. He proceeded on to their planned destination anyway, thinking he would meet him once he arrived at the home of the friend. But Walter did not show up. James retraced his steps and finally came upon a crowd gathered around a singer. Once his ears heard the dulcet tones of the singer, he knew it was his brother Walter. Surprised, because he knew his brother to be a shy young man, he could not help but wonder why in the world Walter would be performing an impromptu concert.

A blind beggar had spent a futile day holding out his hat asking for pennies. "Give a penny to a blind man. Give a penny to a blind man." Near midnight, the crowd quickened its pace, bypassing the beggar. But Walter Scott stopped. His heart was touched by the blind beggar's imploring look. He took his place by the beggar's side and began singing the sweetest of old Scotia's songs—songs few Scots could hear unmoved. At the conclusion of the first song, Walter made an appeal for pennies. A shower of them fell into the hat, not only pennies but silver such as never had fallen into the blind man's hat before. The audience called for another song. Walter granted the request but, as he began to sing, decisively pointed to the hat. He sang on throughout the night. The story touched on the definitive character of Walter Scott. Whenever people heard the story, they nodded in agreement. "Yes, that's the Walter we know."[3]

Walter Scott the artist. We know he was among the accomplished flute players in Edinburgh of his time. We know he was a singer who could move an audience to compassion. He was also a poet. Scott wrote poetry throughout his life, and not infrequently his preaching would take flight on the wings of his own compositions. Here is a sample on the simple subject of "Stars."

What are you, Stars? The eyes of heaven?
Or jewels in God's kingly crown?
Or gems in his imperial robe,
Which he at eventide puts on?
Perhaps you are the military of heaven,
To whom to guard his state the honor's given.

Perhaps you're golden links that bind
The sable curtains of the night,
Or emerald urns, whence flows the die,
That paints them azure when 'tis light;
Or seraph-sentinels round heaven's height,
To watch the sleeping world through the night.[4]

But Walter's art found principal expression as a preacher—the Fred Craddock of the first generation—intelligent, witty, gifted in graciously touching the heart. The beauty of his preaching could come only from one gifted with the heart of an artist. Even that staid, dignified patrician, Alexander Campbell, could not help but get caught up in that kind of preaching. What are the secrets of that kind of gift? That definitive story of Scott and the blind beggar helps uncover the nature of his gift. First, the artist notices, sees what others do not see.

Our common experience is to look but not to see, not to notice, all there is to see. Not Walter Scott. Only the heart of the artist

[3]Dwight E. Stevenson, *Walter Scott: Voice of the Golden Oracle* (St. Louis: Christian Board of Publication, 1946), pp. 20–21.

[4]Ibid., p. 217.

enabled Scott to see the blind beggar with the imploring look. Others looked—by him, through him, around him, over him—but did not see. The heart of an artist sees. Walter Scott could see. He "got it." He saw the wonderful work of the Campbells reforming the church on the basis of New Testament belief and practice. He opened his New Testament and he saw an incomplete picture in the Campbells' ministry. They do wonderful work with, in, and for the church but where is the Pentecost of being afire to preach the Messiah and his promises to the world? Walter Scott's high powers of perception let him make a complementary and fulfilling contribution to the Stone-Campbell reformation.

Scott also noticed the power of art in helping people come to know Jesus Christ. This is particularly illustrated by the story of Scott's singing for the blind beggar. He must have noticed that music, not information (here is a blind person who needs money), moved people to respond with compassion. Music always played a prominent role in his evangelistic work. He traveled with a singing evangelist, William Hayden, a song leader and soloist. Scott said, "It is the office of a hymn to arouse impassioned devotional feelings, even as it is the office of teaching to illuminate understanding."[5]

Scott the artist had the gift of knowing the way artists know. He could see what others could not see. That gift often comes at a very high price. Sensitivity in perception often means pain. Scott got it from his parents; his father was an artist, a music teacher. But pain through sensitivity must have come even more intensely through his mother, Mary. Scott's father, Mary's husband, died very suddenly in a neighboring town. When Mary received the news, she was so stricken she died immediately afterward. Husband and wife, Walter's parents, were buried at the same time, in the same grave.[6]

A glimpse of Scott's sensitivity was exhibited in his shyness. It could also be seen in his alternating moods of manic engagement and debilitating depression. It is unjust to any figure to practice medicine without a license—particularly from the distance of 150 years. But after reading of Scott's life, one should be permitted to raise the question, if not to conclude, that he may have suffered from manic depression.

---

[5]Walter Scott, *Christian Psalms and Hymns (with an addition by Silas W. Leonard, teacher of vocal music, with names of Appropriate Tunes)* (Louisville: J. Maxwell, Jr., 1839, printed by A. S. Tilden, Jeffersonville, Iowa), p. v.

[6]Baxter, p. 30.

Scott had the ability to envision life as it could be and to pursue that new reality with powerfully driven energy. This energy gained expression through his efforts to establish schools and through his ability to devote his total engagement when he wrote books. The supreme illustration of his energetic efforts, of course, rests in the story of his years as an evangelist on the Western Reserve.

There is also plenty of evidence for the other side of his mood, his tendency toward depression. There is melancholy in the story of his lonely search as a young man to seek his place, his purpose, and persons to be his companions in his life's journey. There is evidence of deep pain when Scott experienced early on the rejection of his message. There is even gloom and debilitation in the letdown after three frenzied years of preaching on the Western Reserve. Depression is clearly evident when he and Alexander Campbell have a five-year-long public dispute. Scott simply wanted recognition for his original contribution in identifying the ancient gospel. Campbell rebuffed him. Campbell's rejection of Scott's claims obviously affected the sensitive Walter Scott.

The depression is probably most intense in his heartbreak over the Civil War. He described it clearly in a letter he wrote to his son.

> You say: "I am so disheartened and cast down, so overwhelmed with the general gloom that overspreads my dear, my native land, that I can scarcely think of anything else." These words, my son, precisely describe my state of mind. I can think of nothing but the sorrows and dangers of my most beloved adopted country. God is witness to my tears and grief. I am cast down. I am afflicted, I am all broken to pieces. My confidence in man is gone. May the father of mercies show us mercy. Mine eye runneth down with grief.[7]

Like his mother before him, this sensitive soul could not survive so great a sadness. He died shortly afterward of nothing more apparent than grief.

Alexander Campbell praised Scott for being his most important partner in the reformation except for his father. He wrote very honestly at Scott's death of Scott's depressions and of their time of antagonism.

---

[7]Ibid., p. 441.

> He, indeed, possessed, upon the whole view of his character, a happy temperament. It is true, though not a verb, he had moods and tenses as men of genius generally have. . . I knew him well. I knew him long. I love him much. We might not, indeed, agree in every opinion, nor in every point of expediency; but we never loved each other less because we did not acquiesce in every opinion and in every measure. By the eye of faith and the eye of hope, methinks, I see him in Abraham's bosom.[8]

Scott paid a painful price for possessing the sensitivity which is often part of having the heart of an artist. The artist notices even to the degree of often being painfully sensitive.

The artist also is passionate about communication. Like the poet-prophet Jeremiah, Scott possessed a driving compulsion to connect other persons with the truth he believed he had the privilege to see. These are the two primary gifts of the artist: to see and to communicate what one has seen. The passionate need to communicate often drives the artist to innovation and even to eccentric tendencies. Our beloved founder was no exception. Standing on a street corner, singing one's heart out in the open air as the clock strikes midnight, is both innovative and eccentric at the same time. One might also add that it was effective. An eyewitness of Scott's preaching describes one particularly eccentric and innovative scene:

> Mr. Scott was often eccentric; but he possessed the talent to sustain himself and turn his eccentricity to good account. On one occasion, when the whole country around was almost tremulous in anticipation of hearing him, he managed to slip into the assembly unobserved, and seating himself far back, with his cloak well about his face, and his broad-brimmed hat well drawn down, he sat listening to the remarks of the assembling multitude…
>
> One man says, in a low tone: "What do you think of Scott?" without waiting a reply, "I never heard such a preacher; he is hard on the sects, but he has the Bible on his tongue's end."

[8]Ibid., pp. 448–449.

> Another: "I never read such things in the Bible as he is telling us." His quick ear was catching these "droppings" of the people. The room became packed.
>
> "Do you think the preacher is coming?"
>
> Then rising to full position, still sitting on his seat, laying back his cloak and removing his hat, Scott cried out in his magnificent voice, "And what went ye out into the wilderness to see? A reed shaken with the wind? But what went ye out to see? A man clothed in soft raiment? But what went ye out to see? A prophet? Yea, I say unto you, and more than a prophet."
>
> Then with a sweep, and brilliancy, and point that astonished and instructed all, he discoursed on the ministry of John the Baptist; the preparation of the gospel; the introduction of Jesus by him to the Jewish nation; and carried his audience up to the crucifixion, the resurrection and coronation of the Lord of glory, and the descent on Pentecost of the Holy Spirit, with the grand events of the "notable day of the Lord." It is needless to pause and describe the wonderful effect of this sudden outburst and powerful rehearsal of the gospel upon his astonished auditors.[9]

What can today's Christians learn from Scott about how they learn of God as they move beyond the Enlightenment, the Age of Reason? Scientific learning values skepticism, distance, objectivity, and reason. The artist, however, knows through faith, intimacy, commitment, and affection. Scott somehow combined the two approaches, utilizing the best of the artistic personality. The artist guides our learning not by skepticism but faith, not by distance but intimacy, not by objectivity but commitment, and not by reason alone but with informed affection.

Hear Scott's answer to an important question he asked himself at the College of Teachers and Western Literary Institute in Cincinnati in 1837. What is it that the teacher may develop in the nature of his pupil?

> I answer, certain cardinal virtues [such] as the love of truth, taste, or love of the useful and the beautiful, the love of

[9]Stevenson, pp. 82–83.

our own species, the love of God; elements of virtuous character.[10]

The word love is not a word of distant detachment, but the most intimate of all words. Scott instructs Christians to move from detachment to intimacy, to commitment, to virtue.

A few days after the firing on Fort Sumter, the spark that ignited the Civil War, Scott wrote, "Alas, for my country! Civil war is now most certainly inaugurated, and its termination who can foresee? Who can predict? Twice has the state of things filled my eyes with tears this day. Oh! my country! My country! How I love thee! How I deplore thy present misfortunes!" In about a week, this able-bodied but grief-stricken 64-year-old man was dead.

Through his art, this educator-preacher drew people into an intimate knowing of God. He was an artist, formed and affected by his own words. No doubt his own art comforted him as he drew closer to the presence of God. This son of Scotland, and gifted artist to America, may have been caught up in the music of his own voice when he earlier described the Christians' journey home. As related by William Baxter:

> [Scott] cried out: "[The gathering of the saints in their final glorious home] reminds me of a scene in the mountains of my native north," and then dashed off into a life-like description of the gathering of the clans in the Highlands of Scotland at the call of some renowned and beloved chief. On a mountain summit stood the chiefton [*sic*], and as the wild notes of the buglehorn, re-echoed from rock and ravine, and spread over the valley, the whole plain below was, in a moment, filled with his devoted followers, who wrapped in their plaids, had been concealed in the blooming heather; every eye in that host was turned to the chief whose summons they had heard, and whose form stood out clearly defined on the mountain top, and upward to him in a living stream they went; he shouted a welcome as they came, and back from the thronging host came an answering shout, for they were not only his soldiers but his kinsmen; and when they reached the place where their leader stood they were happy and invincible.[11]

---

[10]Baxter, p. 366.
[11]Ibid., p. 344.

INTRODUCTION

Walter Scott: A Nineteenth-Century Evangelical

Mark G. Toulouse

The name of Walter Scott has long been known among historians of the Stone-Campbell Movement. But general knowledge of the man has been limited mostly to his early reputation as an evangelist for the movement. His passionate work among the unchurched proved crucial to the growth, health, and vitality of the early Christians on the American frontier. But, as these essays demonstrate, there is so much more to the life and thought of the man who lived long past his actual evangelistic crusades on the Western Reserve (1827–1830). Scott died in 1861, more than thirty years after the evangelistic work for which he is mostly remembered. His legacy is more complex than most people have realized. And it serves as an excellent example of the vibrant interaction between culture and faith.

The written work covering his life has not been extensive, especially when compared to the numbers of pages devoted particularly to the life and work of, say, Alexander Campbell and Barton Stone. The authors of these pages have certainly relied upon the fine work of those who have written biographies of Scott in the past (from William Baxter in the 1870s to Dwight E. Stevenson in the 1940s to William Gerrard in the late 1980s). A perusal of the footnotes of these essays will point the interested reader in the direction of those who laid the foundation upon which these writers have built. But they have uncovered new aspects of Scott's character as well. The advantage of a multiauthor work like this one rests precisely in the multitude of perspectives these various writers bring to the topic at hand. These essays, taken together, paint an interesting portrait of the man, one simply unavailable in print until now.

I have always believed Scott's journalistic endeavors serve as an introduction to the diversity of his interests. His writing and editing during those years (1832–1850) reveals a wide, and somewhat eclectic, range of interests. He wrote regularly on all the theological themes of the Stone-Campbell Movement. But he also had other favorite topics. The first three essays, for example, in his first issue of *The Evangelist* were titled "Bible," "Christianity," and "Swearing." Those three essays were of equal length. The first two topics possessed an obvious Stone-Campbell flavor. But "swearing"? "Can nothing be done," wrote Scott, "to put down the unlimited and appalling profanation of God's most holy name practised [*sic*] in our land every where, from the Lakes to Mexico, from the Ocean to the Mississippi?" As a matter of fact, Scott had an interest in stemming the tide of swearing throughout his journalistic life.[1]

This interest reflected the concern of nearly all the nation's nineteenth-century evangelicals to address the topic of the nation's morality, or lack thereof. Most often they expressed it through giving special attention to the personal morality of the nation's citizens. Social or corporate sin was only rarely present in their theological repertoire. Scott, through his journalistic work, offers a good example of the evangelical mind in this respect. "Drinking and cursing are crying sins in Ohio," he wrote (Oh, for the time, the modern reader might lament, when drinking and swearing were the major sins we had to worry about!).[2] In 1838, he recorded the vote of his local church not to have Christian communion with anyone involved in the selling of alcohol, "except for medicine or the Lord's supper." Scott could write as good an evangelical diatribe

---

[1]"Swearing," *The Evangelist* (2 January 1832): p. 5; see, for example, "Profane Swearing," *Protestant Unionist* (11 June 1845): p. 106; "Swearing" (10 June 1846): p.106; "Profanity" (1 December 1847): p. 208.

[2]*The Evangelist* (1 August 1838): p. 191.

as the next person when it came to the individual sins of the nation's citizens, whether pertaining to the consumption of alcohol or the failure to maintain traditional family discipline or the "unmannerly practice" of "unfeeling brethren" who chew tobacco during church meetings and spit on the floor or on the walls. His attention to sin in general, however, must not be taken to mean he thought human beings to demonstrate the truth of the doctrine of "total depravity." Such an idea, he wrote, "owes its origin wholly to the disturbed imagination of crazy theologues."[3]

On the complex subject of slavery, with its economic and political ramifications standing alongside the divisions within the church about the topic, Scott could find no prophetic word to offer. When, in 1834, Nathaniel Field wrote that his church had "resolved not to *break the loaf* with slaveholders, or in any way to countenance them, as Christians," Scott did not mince words in his reply. Even though Scott did not defend slavery, he recognized that many Christians, especially in the South, depended heavily upon slaveholding. He advocated the gradualist approach to ending it. His reply to Field offered a clear chastisement: "Who ordered your church of seventy members at Jeffersonville to make laws for herself...?"[4] Evidently, Scott believed laws restricting Christian communion could be established in one area (alcohol) but not in another (slavery). More important, I suppose, is the point that slavery wrought havoc among most evangelical groups in America. Disciples, as illustrated by the correspondence between Scott and Field, were not immune to these divisions.

Scott's writing does demonstrate a long-standing support for the empowerment of women. When speaking of the 120 disciples at Pentecost, Scott went out of his way to remind his readers that "women were endowed with power from on high as well as men." The Bible is clear on that point. "Philip," he told his readers, "had daughters who prophesied."[5] He supported the work of women as "Deaconesses" in the church and extolled the virtue of their work

---

[3]On the church of Carthage vote, see *The Evangelist* (January 1838): p. 22; for condemnation of consumption of alcohol, see, for example, "Drunkenness," *The Evangelist* (1 July 1833): p. 167; ibid. (1 September 1838): p. 209; "The Ravages of Rum," *Protestant Unionist* (4 December 1844): p. 23; and "Total Abstinence," *Protestant Unionist* (1 March 1848): p. 50; on family discipline, see "Family Discipline," *The Evangelist* (1 October 1838): pp. 223–224; on tobacco, see the letter from E. M. and the response from Scott, *Protestant Unionist* (22 September 1947): p. 166; on the doctrine of total depravity, see "Dialogue," *The Evangelist* (8 July 1834): pp. 151–153.

[4]See the exchange between Nat Field and Scott, *The Evangelist* (6 October 1834): pp. 233–236.

[5]See "Answer," *The Evangelist* (3 June 1833): pp. 142–144.

on behalf of the poor.[6] Further, Scott consistently stressed the importance of education for women and, among early Disciples, especially supported the development of the so-called "female institutes" specializing in providing a well-rounded education for women.[7] "So completely have the talents of women been kept down," complained one editorial, "that there is scarcely a single work, either of reason or imagination, written by a woman, which is in general circulation."[8] Within a few years, of course, Harriet Beecher Stowe wrote *Uncle Tom's Cabin*, a book that took the country by storm.

Scott's belief in women's education did not translate into support for their right to be employed outside the home. Women belonged at home, keeping the home fires burning for their husbands and inculcating the piety of the family:

> But where in life is her loveliness more appreciated, or her excellence better felt, or the compliment of her destiny so completely filled up, as when at home she is seen, at early morn or dewy eve, a christian wife approaching the beloved and honored subject of her heart's dearest affections—her own husband—with the book of God, the holy Bible in her hand, that he may read and pray...This is the true glory of the United States.[9]

In another location, Scott urged the wife "to obey [the husband] in all things; to win him to piety, and raise for him 'a godly seed.'" His instructions to women were usually accompanied by instructions to men in good evangelical fashion: "He is to love his wife alone...to provide for her; to impart to her instruction;...to love her, as Christ loves the church."[10] Throughout the publication life of *The Protestant Unionist*, Scott included in every issue a section of the paper dedicated to the "Family Circle." It contained

---

[6]For example: *The Evangelist* (1 March 1840): p. 72.

[7]"Female Collegiate Institute at Georgetown," ibid. (May 1838): p. 120; "Family Discipline," ibid. (1 October 1838): pp. 223–224; James Evans, "Letter to Scott," ibid. (1 March 1839): pp. 58–60; "Female Institute, Georgetown, Ky." ibid. (1 June 1840): pp. 137–138; "Female Atheneum," and "Poplar Hill Female Seminary, Kentucky," ibid. (1 August 1840): p. 192; "Hygaean Academy," ibid. (1 November 1842): pp. 263–264; or "Kentucky Female Orphan School," *Protestant Unionist* (27 October 1847): p. 186.

[8]"Female Education," ibid. (12 November 1845): p. 196.

[9]"The Christian Wife At Home," ibid. (25 September 1844): p. 4.

[10]"Marriage," ibid. (8 January 1845): p. 41.

little bits of wisdom to enrich and defend the status quo of American family life.

Scott never tired of giving advice concerning the "character" of church life as well. Among other things, he urged congregations to provide life sustaining wages for their preachers and evangelists. "To enrich preachers," Scott warned, "is highly dangerous to the purity of christianity; but to do our labouring brethren a sheer and palpable injustice by sending for them to labour among us one, two, and three days without remuneration, is highly dangerous to our character before God."[11] He could also turn his concern to the character of the evangelist as well. When L. L. Pinkerton temporarily returned to the sole practice of medicine because he could not support himself on funds derived from his ministry, Scott intoned:

> I think it still more necessary that our Evangelists themselves reflect upon the sacred nature of the obligations they incur when they enter the field of evangelical labor. I can find no apology for any capable person's retiring from the work of the Lord. Is it possible that he that feeds the ravens will not feed his choice men...Let the estimable person spoken of in your letter...return to the office for which he is so admirably fitted, and trust in the Lord his God.[12]

As is well-known, Scott had a keen interest in the evangelistic preaching being done in the church and considered himself not only a preacher, but a teacher of preachers. In 1840, he published a comprehensive grading of some of the evangelists in the church, using only the first letter of their name. They were graded according to established categories making it easy to compare one to another. Examples of two very different preachers, one, a young and promising evangelist who gained praise, and the second, an evangelist who needed to improve, give the reader a good feel for how this evaluative process worked:

---

[11]"On Church Character," *The Evangelist* (5 August 1833): pp. 169–171; see also "Law of Ministerial Support," *Protestant Unionist* (1 January 1845): p. 37.

[12]Response to a letter from James Pomeroy, *The Evangelist* (1 March 1840): pp. 71–72; see also "Evangelists," ibid., pp. 62–63.

Ev. Young K______.

Quality of Voice—excellent bottom, firm, full. *Articulation*—labial and decided. *Enunciation*—free, and fast and slow alternately. *Emphasis, Pause, Tone*—silvery. *Action*—firm, and indicative of benevolence, sincerity, and piety. *Language*—good. *Logic* and *Rhetoric*—undecided. *Oratory*—that of the heart and affections, beautiful, sparkling, impressive, and bespeaking wondrous and divine modesty in the orator. Genius is full of imitation; brother K—look at the best models, and improve, but don't mimick [*sic*] them.

Ev. M______.

Quality of Voice—thin, wiry, nasal, and without volume. *Articulation*—imperfect. *Enunciation*—hurried and slow alternately, occasionally screaming. *Emphasis*—breaking rudely upon certain words. *Pause*—indicative of self-esteem. *Tone*—sarcastic. *Action and motions*—cold, affected, indicating large imitation. *Language*—good, but occasionally egotistical. *Logic*—proposition and proof. *Rhetoric*—homely, pointed but not brilliant, curious but not impressive. *Eloquence*—that of reason rather than feeling, and of the head rather than the heart. Much light, little heat, the light of the sun with the coldness of the moon united. When M_____shall see that oratory is an art as well as a science, intended to persuade as well as to convince, to move the will as well as illuminate the understanding, and to compel to duty as well as to impart knowledge; when his voice shall have acquired greater volume and his *ensemble* display less self-complacency, less imitation, he will be *ipse agmen* a host in himself…he should practice vocalization.[13]

Well known as a preacher who could preach for long periods of time, Scott had little patience when the preacher's sermon outlasted the ideas it contained: "The only difficulty which he seems

[13]"Public Speakers," ibid. (1 May 1840): pp. 110–112; see also "Public Speakers," (1 June 1840): pp. 130–131.

to labor under is to get his intellectual machinery, when once under full way, to stop when the grist is out."[14]

Another aspect of evangelical church life Scott often wrote about in his life as a journalist was the church's music ministry. He urged the "cultivation of sacred music" as one of the "potent means appointed by God, confirming the professors of religion in their most holy faith." He praised the Lutherans as "the best singers in the world," with the Episcopalians second. The Presbyterians and the Baptists were making great strides. Scott set about enlarging the hymnbook he and Alexander Campbell had produced earlier until it contained around 700 hymns. Campbell refused to put his name on the enlarged hymnal until it passed muster with a committee of "the brethren." In the meantime, Scott expended three hundred dollars of his own money to get it published and distributed under his own name.[15] He hoped, through the hymnal, to encourage congregations to stop "the endlessly repeated singing of the same hymn to the same tune, at present so common in our assemblies." His hymnbook contained a "Gospel Department" made up of the "most affecting pieces" he could find. Of course, these hymns were divided according to Scott's elements of the true gospel: faith, repentance, baptism, remission of sins, the Holy Spirit, and eternal life.[16]

Throughout his years at *The Evangelist,* Scott pursued a number of regular theological themes. He wrote often of the primitive church, the ancient gospel, church union, and baptism. Discussions on the nature and character of the Messiah showed up regularly. Through 1840 and 1841, he wrote an extensive series on Christian perfection and featured another series on Christian discipline. During 1841, he wrote five essays exposing the problems of the Mormon Bible and detailing the history of that movement. From the late 1830s to the early 1840s, Scott turned an increasing portion of his attention to the second coming of Christ, taking a special interest in the prophecies of William Miller who predicted the end of the world by March 21, 1844, and, finally after recalculation, by October 22, 1844. Once the date had passed, Scott largely set such rumination aside.

In the fall of 1844, Scott turned his attention to publishing the *Protestant Unionist*. He set himself on a weekly publishing schedule

[14]Quoted in "Long Sermons," *Protestant Unionist* (13 November 1844): p. 10.

[15]"Sacred Music," *The Evangelist* (1 August 1839): p. 191; on the details of the new hymnal, see "Our Hymn Book Improved," ibid., pp. 191–192.

[16]"Preface to the Hymn Book," ibid. (1 December 1839): pp. 276–279.

producing a new paper every Wednesday. This demanding schedule occupied a majority of his time in the next few years. The "prospectus" of the paper sounded appropriately Disciple-like with its devotion to "the development and advocacy of Original Christianity, as exhibited on the pages of the New Testament Scriptures, unmixed with human traditions or institutions." Scott described the paper as a "family newspaper."[17] It dealt with contemporary events across the world, devoting sections to both domestic and foreign news. In its pages, one finds coverage of various and sundry items, including the Mexican-American War of 1845 ("Mexican people are now our enemies")[18]; the stories of the territories as they became states (Texas, Oregon, California); and the yellow fever outbreak in New Orleans. The careful reader will find Scott editorializing on behalf of the death penalty and against the American practice of dueling.[19]

One would have to define the major stance of the paper to be "anti-Catholic." In this position, Scott modeled the concerns of much of nineteenth-century evangelicalism in America. The rapid growth of Catholicism during the first half of the century greatly concerned Protestant Christians. Catholicism, Scott wrote, is "making such fearful advances in this nation."[20] These advances, in his opinion, threatened the heart of the nation itself. "Popery is utterly hostile to the rights guaranteed to us, by the Constitution of the United States."[21] The effects of "idolatry, Mohametism, and Catholicism" were disastrous for any country. "We are constrained to avow it as our solemn judgment," said Scott, "that Protestantism, by which we mean the Bible, is the only hope of the nations."[22] Thus, for Scott, Christian union obviously meant "Protestant and Christian, rather than papistical and Roman…not unity of church membership, but unity of character."[23] In these years, Scott faced criticism from other Disciples that he had abandoned their cause and had taken up the task of Protestantism in general. Some accused Scott of seeking "a Protestant basis on which to place the christian Church." Scott replied that "in reality I am advocating the christian basis on which to plant the Protestant church."[24]

[17]"Prospectus," ibid. (25 September 1844): p. 4.

[18]"War: The Duty of Christians," ibid. (10 June 1846): p. 106.

[19]See "Imposters," ibid. (7 July 1847): 122; and "Duelling Murder," ibid. (22 September, 1847): p. 163.

[20]"To Our Subscribers," ibid. (22 January 1845): p. 50.

[21]"The Pope's Encyclical Letter," ibid. (6 November 1844): p. 6.

[22]"To Our Subscribers," ibid. (22 January 1845): p. 50.

[23]"Union," ibid. (25 September 1844): p. 1.

[24]P. 292.

Jacob Creath, Jr., a minister among Disciples, asked Scott directly whether he still believed that the ancient gospel he had once preached (composed of faith, repentance, baptism for the remission of sins, the gift of the Holy Spirit, and the hope of eternal life) remained the only basis of union. Scott's reply is interesting because it reveals he had some second thoughts about the role his "five-finger exercise" played in the history of the Disciples of Christ. Scott replied that he still believed the ancient gospel to be the true source of union, but he felt like his plea for the ancient gospel had been watered down into a simplistic formula that had made it too easy to miss altogether the profound basis upon which the ancient gospel had always rested: the proclamation of faith in Jesus Christ as the Son of God.

> Our main thought at that time was to push back the christian profession on to its original basis—the Messiah. We did this, and the people were received to the remission of sins on the primitive faith of Jesus as the Son of God. But although this was the actual and practical restoration of the central truth in our religion to its proper place in the christian system, many failed nevertheless to see it, and were carried away wholly by the easier and more popular generalization of faith, repentance, baptism, &c., till, in fact, they do not know their own principles when they are advocated.[25]

Creath put the question in yet another way. "Does Brother Scott now propose the same plan of union that he did then, or less, or more?" Scott assured Creath that he proposed "the same without any increase or diminution whatsoever." And in amplifying his answer, he provided a summary of what proved to be the core theological concern throughout Scott's life, something found in one form or another in all the essays of this book:

> We have chosen this truth as the central thought of our own religion—that our Redeemer is the Son of the living God; and have propounded it as such to other men for their adoption because we are sure that God our heavenly Father did it before we did it; and because we feel the necessities of our nature require it.[26]

[25]Ibid.
[26]Ibid.

Given this self-understanding, one might think that Scott saw himself as the Paul of the Disciples, the one who spread the truth of the gospel far and wide. Interestingly, Scott described Campbell as the Paul of the movement. Campbell, like Paul, was the theologian of the movement, complete with "his voluminous writings." By his description of what Campbell was not, it is fairly obvious that Scott cast himself in the role of Peter.

> But although it did not fall to the lot of Mr. Campbell to propound the greatest truth in our religion to society for its proper purposes, and thereupon rectify all the first principles of the kingdom of God; although it was not given him to restore the original advocacy of the gospel, and by this advocacy cut out from among the innumerable sectaries with which christendom swarms a new people with new knowledge and new manners and customs and place them on the exclusive and infallible basis of the Messiahship alone, saved, justified and sanctified; although he was not called in our reformation by Divine Providence to set the part of Peter as one may say, and encounter the shame and insult and difficulties associated with the almost superhuman and protracted and personal effort for years necessary to re-establish the kingdom of God as at the beginning, yet he has doubtless, by Divine Providence been invited to the performance of a certainly no less distinguished work—the work of Paul.[27]

Throughout his life, Scott tended to feel that the movement had neglected the role he had played in restoring the ancient gospel and nurturing the Disciples toward union with other Christians. Though Campbell and Scott remained friends throughout their lives, Scott often felt that Campbell's ego caused him to claim the only significant role in the history of the nineteenth-century Christian reformation. It was Campbell who usually found himself the focal point of controversy. So much was this the case that, by the early 1840s, the early reformers were known as "Campbellites," a name first used to describe them by, according to Scott, the "notorious Reverend Lawrence Graterake." Scott informed his readers that Graterake labored under "historical error on the point." "It is not the 'Disciples' that are Campbellites," wrote

[27]Ibid.

Scott, "but Mr. Campbell that is a 'Disciple.'"[28] Scott hoped someday that someone would provide a more complete history of the Disciples, one including the "acts of Peter."

> Thus as of old we have our Pauls and Peters, but any history of our reformation not embracing the work of the latter as well as that of the former, will always be like the "Acts of the Apostles" with the acts of Peter left out...[29]

This book constitutes our attempt to tell a more complete story of "Peter" and his long-lasting role in the movement. As was true of the Biblical Peter, this story is not always a complementary one, but it is always respectful of both the man and the history he lived. And it describes a multitalented and multidimensional man of his times. In these pages is told the story of Scott the artist; the Jacksonian American and Protestant crusader; the Scottish Presbyterian turned American reformer; the anti creedalist with a creed of his own; the non theologian, as legend would have it, who actually, legend be hanged, was a theologian; the Reformed theologian who, in spite of his hefty criticisms of Calvin, sounded a good deal like him in many ways; the biblical theologian whose study of the Bible followed Scottish theology more than Scottish philosophy; the rationalist who, nevertheless, possessed a sincere and pietistic and deeply genuine spirituality; and, of course, the evangelist and the preacher. All this and more, this story is about Walter Scott, a nineteenth-century evangelical.

---

[28]"Names," *Protestant Unionist* (21 February 1848): p. 46.

[29]Reply to Jacob Creath, *Protestant Unionist* (1 November 1847): p. 190. For a discussion of previous disagreements between Scott and Campbell on Scott's role in the early history of the movement, see Toulouse, *Joined in Discipleship: The Shaping of Contemporary Disciples Identity* (St. Louis: Chalice Press, 1997), chapter 5, "The Eschatological Principle: God With Us," footnotes 29–31.

CHAPTER ONE

Walter Scott and the Nineteenth-Century Evangelical Spirit

David Edwin Harrell, Jr.

The American political revolution concluded on March 4, 1829, when the White House was invaded by General Andrew Jackson and an untidy army of westerners, a democratic uprising, thwarted four years earlier by an ostensibly "corrupt bargain" between John Quincy Adams and Henry Clay, and was of enormous symbolic importance. Privilege and pomp had been routed; nothing seemed to stand before the united will of the people. The young nation was enthralled by its richness, grandeur, destiny, and greatness; cities were mushrooming, invention was blooming, factories were building; optimism and change were in the air. All things seemed possible and within reach of the common citizen.

During the Age of Jackson, preachers, prophets, and social reformers were as abundant and as colorful as the flora and fauna of the virgin land. In 1827, the year that Walter Scott restored the ancient gospel while serving as evangelist for the Mahoning

Association, other auspicious religious events were taking place. Charles Granison Finney was using "new methods" to bring thousands of sinners to the "anxious bench" and raising organized revivalism to new heights, and, in the same year, Joseph Smith began translating the plates shown to him by the Angel Moroni. By the 1830s startling discoveries, revelations, and social elixirs were being marketed in America like patent medicine—by Shakers, spiritualists, socialists, utopians, abolitionists, transcendentalists, feminists, and by countless preachers, both orthodox and exotic.

Since the pioneering books by Alice Felt Tyler, *Freedom's Ferment*, published in 1944, and by Whitney R. Cross, *The Burned-Over District*, published in 1950, American social and religious historians have been well aware of the extraordinary fertility of Jacksonian soil for sprouting social and religious "ultraism."[1] In hindsight, it would have been remarkable had someone not restored the ancient gospel during these most creative of American times. Scott's biographer William A. Gerrard, III noted: "For the nation, her new religions and the revivalists, and for Walter Scott especially, 1827 was a high point."[2] For the Finney converts in Rochester, and the Garrison zealots in Boston, the magical year was 1831; Jacksonian America was, in truth, a season of memorable years.

It is a truism to state that Walter Scott was a man of his time. The Disciples of Christ were a people of their time. "An environmental determinist," Ronald Osborn observed, "could readily interpret their venture as an ecclesiastical and theological parallel to the national political experience."[3] Winfred Garrison long ago utilized the most appropriate subtitle for a history of the Disciples of Christ—"An American Religious Movement." One can argue that Walter Scott was the most American among the early Disciples leaders; his three major shifts of interests were dictated by national events and moods rather than by the internal dynamics of Disciples history.

A political admirer of Jefferson and Jackson, Walter Scott drank deeply of the ethos of Jacksonian democracy.[4] Like his fellow

---

[1]See Alice Felt Tyler, *Freedom's Ferment* (Torchbooks ed.; New York: Harper & Row, Publishers, 1965) and Whitney R. Cross, *The Burned-Over District* (New York: Harper & Row, 1950).

[2]William A. Gerrard III, *Walter Scott* (N. p.: College Press Publishing Company, 1992), p. 18.

[3]Ronald E. Osborn, *Experiment in Liberty* (St. Louis: The Bethany Press, 1978), p. 21.

[4]William Baxter, *Life of Elder Walter Scott* (Cincinnati: Bosworth, Chase & Hall, Publishers, 1874), p. 352.

citizens in the 1830s, Scott assumed that all of human history had been proceeding toward the New World where Americans were creating a nation unexcelled in the arts, scientific prowess, and religious purity. For Scott, as for other Jeffersonians, the foundation of American superiority was "a national system of schools with well-trained teachers."[5] During the euphoric early years of the restoration movement, Scott's self-evaluations ranged from the grandiose to the absurd. His report to the Mahoning Association in 1827, rightly called "typical of the man" by Henry K. Shaw, placed his year's labors in a context that included the millennium, "Mohomet," the pope, the inquisition, French atheism, and freedom of religion in America.[6]

Whatever the topic, Scott was likely to launch into grandiloquent historical summaries that moved unswervingly from "the invention of the Mariner's Compass and the Art of Printing" to the "revival of letters and the Discovery of America," to the Protestant Reformation, and finally to the auspicious restoration of the gospel in America.[7] He relished recounting "the labors and attainments of Hus, Jerome, Wickliffe, Luther, Calvin, Melancthon, Wesley, and others"; when he noted, as he frequently did, that "the God of heaven has been raising up a succession of illustrious men" to finish the reformation, one could easily surmise that the latest raising up had been in the neighborhood of Ohio.[8]

In *The Gospel Restored* Scott placed his contribution, along with those of the Campbells, in the narrower restoration context, noting the "three successive steps, which the lovers of our Lord Jesus have been enabled to make, in their return to the original institution: First, the Bible was adopted as sole authority in our assemblies...Next the Apostolic order was proposed. Finally the true gospel was restored."[9] In the first number of *The Evangelist*, Scott staked his claim to a place in the Reformation Hall of Fame: "The restoration of the ancient gospel, forms a new era in the history of reformation...Antecedently to eighteen-hundred and

[5]Quoted in Dwight Stevenson, *Walter Scott: Voice of the Golden Oracle* (St. Louis: Christian Board of Publication, 1946), p. 167.

[6]Henry K. Shaw, *Buckeye Disciples* (St. Louis: Christian Board of Publication, 1952), p. 52.

[7]"The State-System, An Address by Walter Scott, President *pro tem*, of Bacon College, Georgetown, Ky.," *The Christian* (February and March 1837): p. 27

[8]See "Cleansing of the Sanctuary, No. 1," *The Evangelist* (1 May 1840): pp. 19–20.

[9]Walter Scott, *The Gospel Restored* (Cincinnati: Printed by O. H. Donogh, 1836), p. vi.

twenty-seven, no party... seems to have possessed the least practical knowledge of this matter."[10]

Scott believed his restored gospel succeeded because it made Christians rather than sinners recipients of the Holy Spirit, thus rationalizing faith and the conversion process.[11] Scott's restored gospel was a distinctly left-brained alternative offered to a population enthralled by the blossoming of science and rational thought. In 1827 he was the right man in the right place with the right message.

Scott's "true gospel" clashed in the American marketplace with the cornucopia of new ideas being hawked in the 1830s. There were lots of right-brained religious competitors ranging from spiritualism and transcendentalism to Methodism, the greatest of the religious marketers of the nineteenth century. (The Methodist triumph in the nineteenth century should have prepared twentieth-century observers for the prowess of right-brained pentecostal thinking in the modern age of secularism and science.) The true gospel did well by some measures, but fell far short of winning the nation and the world. "I am persuaded that nothing but more zeal in our laborers, more zeal and devotedness in all the disciples, are necessary to make it triumph among men,"[12] Scott insisted in 1832, but human perversity prevailed and millions chose to follow charlatans and fools rather than accept the logic of the true gospel.

Scott was particularly upset by defections to Mormonism, including the departure of Sydney Rigdon. In 1841, he admitted that "our heart sickens" because "we are compelled to admit that by the devices of an apostate brother" the restoration message itself had "been associated with one of the grossest impostures that ever was attempted to be palmed off upon mankind—I mean Mormonism."[13]

Even more deflating to Scott than the limited success his historic discovery had achieved after a decade was the bumpy ride the restored gospel received among his friends. He was stung by Alexander Campbell's criticism of the unmistakable pretentiousness of *The Gospel Restored*, and he was deeply offended by the charge that he had plagiarized from Campbell's arguments in the

---

[10]"Circular Letter," (January, 1832): pp. 17–18.

[11]Many Disciples historians agree. See Winfred E. Garrison, *Christian Unity and Disciples of Christ* (St. Louis: The Bethany Press, 1955), pp. 88–91.

[12]"Circular Letter," *The Evangelist* (January 1832): p. 18.

[13]"Preface," *The Evangelist* (February 1841): p. iv.

McCalla debate in 1823.[14] Scott's embarrassing defense of his breakthrough and of his elevated historical significance in *The Evangelist*, along with a subsequent quarrel with Campbell in 1840 about naming the movement, contributed to the demise of his paper, his return to Pittsburgh in 1844, and, in all likelihood, to some personal reappraisals concerning the epoch-making events of the Jacksonian Age.

Subsequent generations of Disciples have rather consistently recognized Scott as one of the four founding fathers of the movement because he provided an effective evangelistic method which had been lacking and because it was he who gave the impetus which changed a movement for reform within the Baptist churches into a separate religious body, but by 1840 those contributions were not so clear. In that year the disillusioned Scott wrote to Philip Fall: "The thing has not been what I hoped it would be by a thousand miles."[15]

By 1840 many of the schemes and reforms of the 1830s had fallen short of the optimistic hopes of their discoverers. It was becoming less and less certain that the United States would be the agent for introducing an era of worldwide peace and perfection. This growing uncertainty, in part, drew the nation's attention to the prophetic calculations of a Baptist lay preacher, William Miller. In 1831, Miller first presented his projection that Christ would return to earth in 1843, but his idea was not widely publicized until distributed through a Christian Connection newspaper edited by Joshua V. Himes beginning in 1839.

Jonathan A. Butler and Ronald L. Numbers have noted that Miller's followers remained a "limited regional movement with appeal almost exclusively in the northeastern United States," (the number of loyal adventists was estimated at between 30,000 and 100,000), but the adventist movement nonetheless "cast a broad shadow among its contemporaries."[16] Millions of American evangelical Christians believed that Miller's calculations were wrong and dangerous and therefore gave them publicity, but millions of others accepted his view with varying degrees of credulity; very few people were unaware of the prediction as 1843 loomed on the horizon.

---

[14]See Stevenson, *Walter Scott*, pp. 170–185; "Letters of the Events of 1823 and 1827," *The Evangelist* (December 1838): pp. 266–288.

[15]Cited in Stevenson, *Walter Scott*, p. 179.

[16]*The Disappointed: Miller and Millenarianism in the Nineteenth Century* (Bloomington: Indiana University Press, 1987), p. 5.

In his slightly disillusioned state at the end of the decade of the 1830s, Walter Scott was a prime prospect to become a fellow traveler in the adventist movement. Like all ante-bellum evangelicals, Scott used millennial language throughout his career, and, like most evangelicals, he did not distinguish precisely between pre- and postmillennial versions. The general assessment of Butler and Numbers is appropriate for Scott:

> The antebellum American longing for millennial happiness proliferated numerous crusades to reform society and encouraged experiments aimed at perfecting the world...The remarkable continuities between the Millerites and contemporary reformers further blurs the distinction that once prevailed in millenarian studies between pessimistic, catastrophic, and quietist premillennialists and optimistic, progressive, and reformists postmillennialists.[17]

Still, more than any other Disciples leader, Walter Scott was drawn to premillennial speculations from a very early date. In a series entitled "The Cloud," published in *The Evangelist* in 1834, Scott left little doubt about his millennial expectations: "Christ has much work to do, which seems to require his immediate presence and direction; and many purposes to perform and designs to fulfill, which make his coming to earth, and abiding here for a time, highly necessary."[18] It became increasingly clear to Scott that something more cataclysmic than the restoration of the true gospel was required to set the world in order. "We may have recovered the original gospel," he wrote in 1838, but "we have not yet got to the root of the evil." Humanity desperately needed "social improvement"—reform that would rid the world of "antisocial economy, irreligion, and ignorance, and impure schemes of education, originated in the old world."

Surely, God intended for his people to enjoy a society "infinitely superior to one of those miserable things which we call villages, with two taverns, three grogshops, five kinds of Christians, and no meeting house, two squires, one hundred inhabitants, and two-and-forty suits upon the docket, three physicians, thirty patients, six visiting ministers—one Universalist, two Methodists, two Presbyterians, and one Baptist: billiards every day, and a horse race

---

[17]*The Disappointed*, p. xviii.

[18]*The Evangelist* (4 August 1834): p. 174.

on Saturday and Sunday!"[19] The necessary social improvement would be introduced by the millennium: "The whole superstructure of ancient society must be upset or pulled down, and a better order of things substituted." The millennial triumph of political, economic, and educational truth would enable humanity "perfectly to enjoy the true religion, the glorious gospel of the Son of God." In 1838, Scott believed all of this would come to pass "shortly," as history approached the completion of the 1335 days in Daniel's prophecy.[20]

By 1840 Walter Scott was almost totally preoccupied with millennial interpretation. In May, he wrote: "The moment, we are told, is almost come when the authority of men must be displaced by the authority of God alone." Daniel's prophecies, he believed, would be fulfilled by the "middle of the present century."[21] At the end of 1841, Scott enthusiastically announced that "the Lord Jesus is speedily coming in his own proper person, body or flesh from heaven to raise the dead, change the living, reorganize his Kingdom, and spread it in all its grandeur around the world." He urged his fellow Christians to "keep your eye from this time forward on the clouds."[22]

In 1842 Scott's writings indicate he had become fairly strongly committed to the Millerite movement. "Mr. Miller's scheme," he wrote, "is in point of fact the hope of the gospel and differs in no material point from the most orthordox [*sic*] of the great interpreters." It was only in "its chronology that his scheme astounds and astonishes us," Scott admitted.[23] Scott never succumbed to the fatal date-setting millennial disease, nor did he ever completely endorse the Miller calculation, but he came perilously close: "Mr. Miller affirms that this dreadful catastrophe will occur next year—that the present order of things will be arrested in its boasted progress in 1843, and the world come to an end. We will not deny this, and dare not affirm it."[24]

Near the end of 1842, Scott pronounced that "the second coming of Christ is become the truth of the age." He chided his brethren

---

[19]"Social Improvement," *The Evangelist* (July 1838): p. 163.

[20]Ibid.

[21]"Cleansing of the Sanctuary, No. 1," *The Evangelist* (1 May 1840) : p. 97.

[22]"New Government and New Society, Predicted by the Prophets, No. 8," *The Evangelist* (1 October 1841): p. 221.

[23]"Great Concessions of D. Campbell," *The Evangelist* (1 September 1842): p. 205.

[24]Baxter, *Life of Elder Walter Scott*, p. 394.

because, with "few praise worthy exceptions, the mass of those with whom I have conversed on this matter, display an ingorance [*sic*] of the prophetic word, of which this great and flourishing reformation has just caused [*sic*] to be ashamed."[25] According to William Baxter, by this time, Scott "was regarded... as identified with the Second Adventists. He mingled freely with them at their meetings and participated in them, and invited eminent preachers of that faith to Carthage, and afforded them every facility for the presentation of the views to the people."[26]

The failure of Miller's 1843 prediction was followed by a recalculation that set the date of the Lord's return at October 22, 1844 and set up a subsequent "great disappointment." The adventist movement shattered. By 1844 Walter Scott was once again a somewhat vanquished man. In the second number of the first volume of the *Protestant Unionist*, published two weeks after the "great disappointment," he wrote something of a disclaimer, noting that "we have never been able to see with some other men, that the day, or hour, or the year, of Christ's coming and kingdom could be infallibly ascertained from Scripture."[27] Scott remained respectful of Miller, but like many other evangelical fellow travelers, he bid a subdued farewell to his former adventist friends:

> Without the slightest feeling of disrespect for the leaders of the Second Advent movement, then, we nevertheless humbly believe that it were becoming, as it certainly would be safe, for the pious persons who have been pressed into this movement, never again so unhesitatingly to surrender themselves to the dictation of any man on earth, as they have heretofore done to some of their brethren, and to the venerable Mr. Miller in particular.[28]

By the time of the publication of *The Messiahship or Great Demonstration* (1859), Scott had become thoroughly postmillennial, believing that the millennium was a part of "the history of human progress" and would have a "gradual introduction."[29]

Walter Scott's move from Carthage, Ohio, back to Pittsburgh in 1844 may be interpreted symbolically as illustrative of his taking

---

[25] "To the Brethren," *The Evangelist* (1 October 1842): p. 236.

[26] *Life of Elder Walter Scott*, pp. 393–396.

[27] "The Second Adventists," *Protestant Unionist* (November 1844): p. 6.

[28] Ibid., p. 2.

[29] *The Messiahship or Great Demonstration* (Cincinnati: H. S. Bosworth, 1859), p. 335.

a step back in his life and in his thinking. He left behind the evangelistic field where he had unraveled the secret of the restored gospel and where he had feverishly anticipated the second coming of Christ to return to the site of his earliest Protestant searchings for religious truth and Christian union. His new vision in 1844 identified him much more with the rambunctious evangelical Protestantism of the time than with the Disciples of Christ. Disciples historians have had little to say about the meaning of Scott's days as editor of the substantial weekly called the *Protestant Unionist*. His biographer, William Baxter, noted cryptically that the paper was "well supported and did good service, especially in advocating the union of all the people of God on the Bible alone as the rule of faith and practice."[30]

Scott's agile leap from millennial enthusiasm to the Protestant crusade against Roman Catholicism was entirely predictable. The movement of enthusiasts from premillennialism to the various reforms of the 1840s—nativism, anti-Catholicism, abolitionism, temperance, missions, and even feminism—has been well documented by adventist and social reform historians.[31] A man of Walter Scott's background and prejudices quite naturally found himself drawn to the movement, booming by the 1840s, to organize a white, Anglo-Saxon Protestant hegemony. Scott's interest in the Protestant crusade was not new in the 1840s, as his adventism was not simply a reaction to the Miller movement, but the grand cause of Protestantism pressed its way to the fore in his mind both because of his millennial disillusionment and because the Protestant crusade was reaching its zenith by 1844. The American Protective Association had been formed in Philadelphia in 1842 and evangelical clergy flocked to the cause of presenting a united front against Roman Catholic immigration. The Protestant crusade began to lose steam in the late 1840s because of sectarian bickering, although anti-Catholicism remained an important theme in American politics into the 1850s through the Know-Nothing movement.[32]

In the earliest issues of *The Evangelist* Scott identified himself and other Disciples with the cause of Protestantism. Reporting on

---

[30]*Life of Elder Walter Scott*, p. 397. William Thomas Moore wrote: "At the same time he edited a paper, entitled the Protestant Unionist, which did most excellent service for Protestantism as a whole, as well as for the Restoration Movement to which he was specially committed." *A Comprehensive History of the Disciples of Christ* (New York: Fleming H. Revell Company, 1909), p. 418.

[31]See *The Disappointed*, p. xviii.

[32]See Ray Allen Billington, *The Protestant Crusade*, 1800–1860 (New York: The Macmillan Company, 1938).

a written debate between a Catholic and a Presbyterian in 1833, Scott commended the Protestant protagonist: "We are not Presbyterians, but we are Protestants, and feel the divine excellence of that great and glorious maxim in the Reformation, which recognizes in every son of man the inherent right to read and understand the scriptures for himself. May he inflict a wound upon the beast from which he shall never recover within the happy abodes of our Republic."[33] Of course, most early Disciples located their efforts within the Protestant tradition. *The Christian*, launched in Georgetown, Kentucky by Scott and John T. Johnson in 1837, carried on its masthead the slogan: "Devoted to the union of Protestants upon the foundation of the original gospel and the apostolical order of the primitive church."

The relationship of the Disciples with the emerging American WASP establishment was uneasy, in large part because of Scott's heterodox restored gospel. Scott regretted that it was "the very doctrine of our Ancient Gospel" that caused Disciples to be "so shamefully treated by all parties."[34] The Campbell-Purcell debate in 1837 did something to rid the minds of the Protestant clergy of prejudice toward Campbell and other Disciples, but few reformers actively participated in the organized Protestant crusade in the years before the Civil War. By the 1840s many Disciples preachers had settled into a pattern of baiting their sectarian competitors, but Walter Scott was more conciliatory. In *The Messiahship* he wrote: "Conversion and union being the aims of the Reformation, no preacher should lose his precious time by declaiming against the imperfect views of his fellow professors. *Better to win all hearts than cut off all ears.*"[35]

Scott's Pittsburgh venture in journalism placed him squarely in the leading evangelical religious cause of the mid-1840s. He clearly saw the *Protestant Unionist* as an organ in the Protestant crusade. The masthead of the paper boasted the slogan: "The Bible, I Say the Bible Only, is the Religion of Protestants." The paper, Scott announced, would be "truly Protestant"; it would be "unencumbered by those things which it must unavoidably publish were it

[33]"Controversy Between a Catholic and a Protestant," *The Evangelist* (1 April 1833): p. 77.

[34]Ibid.

[35]P. 292.

of a party nature."[36] Scott insisted that it would be "equally imprudent either to magnify differences or despise them," but he believed that among Protestant churches, "the things in which they agree are infinitely more important than those in which they disagree."[37]

Scott's support for the Protestant crusade paralleled that found in other journals dedicated to the cause of Protestant union and Catholic containment. He extolled Luther as "the greatest of men," the leader of the "ranks of pure priests and new philosophers" who had led the way to Protestant modernity, ranks that included "Bacon, Locke, Boyle, Newton, Zingleus [*sic*], Cranmer, Latimer, Knox, Calvin and other bright and shining stars."[38] He endorsed the new Protestant organizations such as the American Protestant Association and the Friends of the Observance of the Lord's Day and pages of the *Protestant Unionist* were filled with typical anti-Catholic fare.[39] Scott believed the nation faced perilous times that demanded the union of Protestants. He wrote in 1852: "All the friends of evangelical Christianity are loudly called on by the times, by the prevalence of infidelity, and the increase of the Papacy to surrender every prejudice to the faith; popularity to principle, party policy to the general interest of the Church of God; and every other inferior consideration to the great duty of Union and the conversion of mankind."[40]

In hindsight, Scott's foray into the cause of Protestant union and anti-Catholicism seems little more than a diversion, a rather irrelevant addendum to his earlier career. By the early 1850s, it became clear once again that this latest grand cause he embraced had lost its luster. On the one hand, orthodox Disciples assailed him and insisted he was trifling with sectarians who needed to believe, repent, and be baptized. Scott rejected as "extravagant" the assertion of one reader that "Protestantism is the parent of more infidelity than any other cause existing," but he had to be on guard against his Disciples brethren.[41] On the other hand, Scott increasingly despaired of persuading Protestant churches to "reform

[36]"Our Paper," *Protestant Unionist* (8 January 1845).

[37]"Union of Protestants," *Protestant Unionist* (8 January 1845): p. 2.

[38]"Luther," ibid. (27 November 1844): p. 1.

[39]See "Union of Protestants," *Protestant Unionist* (8 January 1845): p. 2 and "National Convention of the Friends of the Observance of the Lord's Day," *Protestant Unionist* (11 December 1844): p. 2.

[40]Quoted in Stevenson, *Walter Scott*, p. 206.

[41]"Answer to Elder Du Val," *Protestant Unionist* (17 May 1848): p. 2.

organically."[42] His resignation was shared by other Protestant leaders of the period; the efforts at uniting Protestant evangelicals against Roman Catholicism encountered countless sectarian hazards. By 1850 the antebellum Protestant crusade had pretty well unraveled.[43]

By the time Scott published *He Nekrosis or the Death of Christ* in 1853, a treatise "written for the recovery of the church from sects," he saw the historic role of Protestantism as "altogether provisional."[44] He wrote: "As a whole Protestantism is *weak*. It is...an assemblage of individual sects...It has developed the grandest principles of our religion, but has not sufficiently estimated *union*. It has preferred *doctrines* to union."[45]

The Messiahship or Great Demonstration, judged by Dwight E. Stevenson to be Scott's "greatest work,"[46] was published two years before Scott's death in 1861. The book contained the kind of sweeping and grand summary of human and divine history so typical of Walter Scott. But for all of its reach, *The Messiahship or Great Demonstration* betrayed the sober realism of a man whose achievements had fallen short of his fullest expectations.

Scott's hopes and expectations, like those of other Americans of his generation, had been tempered by time. His premillennial belief had long since been transformed into a gradualist postmillennialism. He still saw the Reformation as God's effort "to restore to mankind, piecemeal, as they were able to bear it, the religion of his Son," but he now believed that "Christianity has to be restored by various degrees."[47] By the 1850s Scott saw little evidence that Protestantism was near to healing its divisions and restoring true Christianity.

He found it difficult to be euphoric about the promise of America in 1859. Scott still believed that "it may be that in the government of the people of the United States we have an historical illustration of the grand prophesy" that the millennium was approaching.[48] Perhaps the sense of destiny he had shared with other westerners in the 1830s had not been completely misguided.

---

[42]Ibid.

[43]See Billington's chapter, "The Period of Decline, 1845–1850, "*The Protestant Crusade*, pp. 245–261.

[44](Cincinnati : Walter Scott Publisher, 1853), p. 46.

[45]Ibid., pp. 98–99.

[46]Walter Scott, p. 215.

[47]*The Messiahship or Great Demonstration* (Cincinnati : H. S. Bosworth, 1859), p. 290.

[48]Ibid., p. 322.

Americans were, Scott wrote, "all Anglo-Saxons—the offspring of the grandest nation on earth—the British nation." They were "the most pious and enterprising, singular and successful pilgrims or adventurers that ever left their native country for a foreign land."[49] But, in 1859, thirty years removed from the discovery of the true gospel and the democratic fervor of Jacksonian America, it was difficult to be an American optimist.

As the Civil War loomed menacingly on the horizon, even Walter Scott had to acknowledge that "two disturbing forces" were "grievously agitating the republic, namely: 1. The Negro. 2. The Papist."[50] Perhaps more than any other first-generation Disciples leader, Walter Scott was a mirror of America. Like most Americans, his religious and political hopes in the 1820s and 1830s were unbounded, but the brightest human and divine aspirations foundered first on the huge influx of German and Irish Roman Catholics that set off waves of nativism and then on the trauma of slavery and the impending sectional crisis. Walter Scott, like many of his generation of Americans, came to the factious and bellicose United States on the eve of secession and war bewildered and somber, an old man who had dreamed impossible dreams and seen misleading visions.

---

[49]Ibid.

[50]Ibid., pp. 332–333.

CHAPTER TWO

An Implicit Creed: Walter Scott and the Golden Oracle

Amy Collier Artman

Christianity in America in the middle of the nineteenth century was a multifaceted and complicated entity. New influences emerged out of the social and political realm as well as out of the changing nature of the church in the American context. Early in the century, America had won its independence from Britain. During the national period that followed, the flush of political autonomy reached the church. Many leaders of newly emerging Christian movements began to call for concurrent religious autonomy.[1] In addition to the postrevolutionary influences, particular philosophical constructs dominated the nineteenth-century mind.

The philosophy of Scottish Common Sense Realism was one of the most influential. Howard Mumford Jones called it no less than "the official academic belief of the period."[2] It consisted of a profound confidence in "the normal human ability to reach

[1]C. Leonard Allen and Richard T. Hughes, *Illusions of Innocence* (Chicago: University of Chicago Press, 1988), p. 105.

[2]Allen and Hughes, *Innocence*, p. 154.

common sense conclusions on which all human life [is] founded."[3] Common Sense Realism was also the lens through which people of that time incorporated the classic philosophical constructs of Lord Bacon. Baconian thought as interpreted by the Common Sense Realists included "a spirited enthusiasm for natural science," as well as a meticulous empiricism founded upon the Realists' extreme confidence in the human senses. Human beings are fully capable of intuiting what is true by means of their common, or human, sense. In addition, the Baconian Realists regarded all abstract concepts and speculation with deep suspicion, and relied instead upon what they considered to be an "inductive accumulation of facts."[4] The impact of this philosophical view on the nineteenth century cannot be underestimated. One must not think, however, that all that was occurring in America at this time was of a rational, analytical character. This also was the age of revivalism.

Revivalism demanded consideration and response from the Christians of this time due to its sweep across the country. The revival experience included an appreciation of religious impulses; extreme emotionalism was common. Believers were, as Nathan Hatch observed, "encouraged to express their faith with fervent emotion and bold testimony."[5] Camp meetings, with their "exciting, inexplicable hysteria"[6] occurred with great frequency on the frontier. The raw, impassioned experiences of these meetings had far-reaching effects on American Christianity. From this mixture of religious democracy, philosophical rationalism, and revivalistic emotionalism emerged movements that sought to walk the uncertain line between rationalism and emotionalism.

Among the leaders of one of these movements were Thomas and Alexander Campbell, Barton W. Stone, and Walter Scott. Although these men were not alone in their ideology and theology, they can serve as representative of a particular strand of Christianity that developed within the peculiarly American setting. As

---

[3]Howard Mumford Jones, "The Influence of European Ideas in Nineteenth-Century America," *American Literature* 7 (1935): quoted in C. Leonard Allen and Richard T. Hughes, *Illusions of Innocence* (Chicago: University of Chicago Press, 1988), p. 154.

[4]Theodore Dwight Bozeman, *Protestants in an Age of Science* (Chapel Hill: The University of North Carolina Press, 1977); quoted in Allen and Hughes, *Illusions of Innocence*, p. 154.

[5]Nathan O. Hatch, *The Democratization of American Christianity* (New Haven: Yale University Press, 1989), p. 58.

[6]William G. McLoughlin, Jr., *Modern Revivalism: Charles Grandison Finney to Billy Graham* (New York : The Ronald Press Company, 1959), p. 22.

"reformers," these men were committed to a rational faith and belief in human reason. They were committed as well to the call for the restoration of the primitive church in order to bring about the advent of the millennium. Walter Scott shared these commitments. He is remembered as the powerful evangelist who was able to communicate with profound efficiency the message often characterized by the slogan "no creed but Christ."

Walter Scott claimed one thing, and one thing only, as his creed: the statement that Jesus is the Messiah, the Son of God. Scott referred to this confession as a creed, and as such was not wholly anticreedal. He was, however, opposed to the claim that any other statement of belief could stand in the place of or be added to the good confession. He rejected any implication that human additions to this creed were necessary in order to enter into Christian discipleship. Scott defined the creed of Christianity as a statement of belief and the thing necessary for salvation. He also, however, described a creed as "the thing preached by the leaders of sects, and the principles governing their preaching."[7] If a creed is a statement of the beliefs necessary for salvation or that which is preached, then Scott's creed must include more than the simple confession of Jesus as the Messiah. Scott preached this, it is true, but never alone.

In the year 1832, in the pages of *The Millennial Harbinger*, Scott published a proposal for a monthly religious paper called *The Evangelist*. Within this proposal are contained what were, for Scott, "the great principles and privileges which originally constituted the gospel." These included the assertion that Jesus the Messiah died for the sins of humanity according to the Bible, was buried and rose again, is now in heaven, and will finally judge the world. In addition, everyone who believes in Jesus and desires to inherit eternal life will be entitled to a personal acquittal of all sins. Sins are remitted in baptism, and the receipt of the Holy Spirit follows. All who receive the gospel in this manner will receive eternal life.[8] In the words of W. E. Garrison, "Mr. Scott would have scorned to adopt the Apostles' (or any other) Creed, but this covered most of it."[9] Scott converted thousands to a Stone-Campbell movement that claimed to be devoid of any creed other than the scriptural creed

---

[7]Walter Scott, *He Nekrosis*, or *The Death of Christ* (Philadelphia: James Challen and Sons, 1857), p. 32.

[8]Walter Scott, "Prospectus of *The Evangelist*," *Millennial Harbinger* (1832): pp. 46–47.

[9]Winfred Earnest Garrison, *Religion Follows the Frontier* (New York and London: Harper and Brothers Publishers, 1931), p. 148.

of the confession of Christ. Yet, as seen above, in Scott's own teaching and preaching he formulated a structure that operated in addition to this confessional statement as a *de facto* creed. This practical structure was the way he communicated what he believed as well as what he expected all Christians to believe. It made up his implicit creed.

Walter Scott used the confession of Jesus as the Messiah as an explicit creed and rejected all other specific creedal formulations. In practice, however, he developed an implicit creed that outlined the duties demanded of any Christian who had confessed the Golden Oracle of Jesus as the Messiah. Those aspects of the implicit creed particularly vital to Scott's thought and teaching include the emphasis on a reasonable faith, baptism for the remission of sins, and the activity of the Holy Spirit. [10] This description of Scott's belief system as implicitly creedal would likely have made him very uncomfortable. His rejection of any creed but Christ constituted a strong part of his theology.

Anticreedalism

Creeds and creedal formulations of belief were common in the churches of nineteenth-century America. The Westminster Confession, the Apostle's Creed, the Nicene Creed, as well as others,[11] served as statements of faith and right belief for the church member and as items of confession for those desiring to enter into the Christian community. Presbyterians and Episcopalians, however, began early on to feel the far-reaching effect on religion of the newly won political liberty. In the post-Revolutionary environment, creeds and the churches that adhered to them became increasingly identified with the Old World of Britain. The citizens of the new country began to reject remnants of the British enemy in any sphere—political, social, or religious. Raccoon John Smith, leader of a group calling itself simply "Christians," said "a nation could exist without a king on its throne and without a clergyman in the

---

[10]William Austin Gerrard III. "Walter Scott: Frontier Disciples Evangelist" (Ph.D. diss., Emory University, Ann Arbor, Michigan: University Microfilms, 1982), p. 107. According to Gerrard, "At Caesarea Phillipi, the keys of the kingdom were given to Peter, and by the keys Scott meant the ideas of faith, repentance, baptism for the remission of sins, and the gift of the Holy Spirit."

[11]Walter Scott, *The Union of Christians and the Death of Christ*, improved edition adelphia: J. Challen and Sons, 1857), pp. 52–55. Scott lists the Apostles' Creed, anasian Creed, and the Nicene Creed, and then disputes the historical au- y and necessity of these as statements that must be confessed in order to lvation.

sacred desk." The people of America preferred the Common Sense/Baconian ideology of an inductive and personal religion and its denial of the need for any other authority than the Bible and human intellect. "A remarkable number of people awoke one morning to find it self-evident that the priesthood of all believers meant just that—religion of, by, and for the people."[12] Anti-creedalism took strong root in this environment.

Groups under the leadership of Elias Smith, James O'Kelly, Barton Stone, and Alexander Campbell were partially defined by a highly developed sense of this independent, common sense approach to religion and faith. They also were defined, as well as named, for their desire to reform the church and return it to its original New Testament purity. For these Christians, creeds as statements of right belief were unnecessary because the people could discern for themselves what was right belief. They were indebted to the worldview shaped by the thinking of Francis Bacon, John Locke, and Isaac Newton. This "triumvirate" produced a cultural world that "form[ed] the framework within which new religious movements such as the Disciples of Christ took shape and definition."[13]

The early Christian reformers, followers of Campbell, had a strong confidence in the Bible and the ability of human reason to discern "all matters necessary to right doctrine and faith."[14] They asserted that the simple truth revealed in scripture was evident to all reasonable people. No creedal statement could usurp the place of the Bible. The confessions of the churches were considered unscriptural and unnecessary for initiation into Christianity. No toleration existed for any strictures placed upon the common human ability to discern logically, and apprehend personally, the teachings of scripture.

Creeds could serve in a limited capacity as items of education and as means of teaching the faith, but the reformers vehemently rejected any implication that they could be held as a final authority. Anticreedalism became a powerful force because these Christians believed the reform of the church necessarily began with the institution of the pure gospel message. As any good reformer knew, the pure message had to be separated from any creedal additions.

---

[12]Hatch, *Democratization*, p. 69.

[13]Kenneth Lawrence, ed., *Classic Themes of Disciples Theology* (Fort Worth: Texas Christian University Press, 1986), p. 102.

[14]Mark G. Toulouse, *Joined in Discipleship: The Maturing of an American Religious Movement* (St. Louis: Chalice Press, 1992), p. 61.

This was the only message that could unite the whole of Christianity.

A solid link existed between the repudiation of creedal statements and the Disciple "plea" for union among all churches. "[These] religious reformers," asserts Jon Butler, "sought to locate Christianity's themes and doctrines, to dispense with the excess baggage of historical theology, and to embrace the new science, all in order to advance mankind and Christianity in a new society and a new age."[15] A new society and a new age: these two hopes served as the impetus behind the anticreedalism of the Stone-Campbell movement. Creeds stood in the way, ultimately, of the second coming of Christ and the consummation of God's plan for humanity. The time frame and plan of action was simple: restore the church to its primitive state of union by means of preaching the Gospel. This restoration of union would result in the evangelization and conversion of the entire world, thereby bringing about the millennium and the return of Jesus Christ. For Scott, the presence of creeds barred this longed-for union. And without union, there could ultimately be no complete salvation. Scott asserted, "The unity of the church must precede the salvation of the world."[16] He had not, however, always held these convictions, and it was not until he came to America that his fervor to teach and preach against creedalism ignited.

A staunchly Scots-Presbyterian father and mother raised their son Walter with the expectation of his entrance into the clergy. An obedient son, Scott agreed to pursue a religious vocation. He attended the University of Edinburgh due to his parent's recognition of his "decided talent," and soon after his matriculation a benevolent uncle called him to America. After a year of teaching and traveling he met George Forrester, president of a small academy in the city of Pittsburgh. Forrester employed Scott as a teacher, and the two soon became good friends and partners in an intensive study of the Bible.[17] Forrester also served as pastor of a small "primitive" Christian congregation. At the invitation of his employer and friend, Scott attended several worship services.

This church was unlike any ever experienced by Scott. Stevenson described Scott's experience: "[Scott] heard no creeds

---

[15]Jon Butler, *Awash in a Sea of Faith : Christianizing the American People* (Cambridge, Mass.: Harvard University Press, 1990), p. 220.

[16]Walter Scott, *The Union of Christians*, p. 61.

[17]William Baxter, *Life of Elder Walter Scott* (Cincinnati: Bosworth, Chase and Hall, Publishers, 1874), pp. 36–38.

recited. The service was simple and, wherever possible, in the language of scripture...Here was a church determined to be guided by nothing that it could not find in the letter of the Bible. It was a 'Haldane' church."[18] Haldane churches were congregations founded upon the beliefs of the Haldane brothers who came to America from Scotland. The Haldanes advocated the weekly observation of the Lord's supper and the restoration of the primitive order of the church as outlined in the New Testament. Baptism by immersion developed later within Haldane congregations in America, and was practiced by the Forrester congregation.[19] As Scott continued to attend the church and to study under the tutelage of Forrester, he came to question much of his Presbyterian upbringing.

The newness of the Haldane teachings energized and amazed Scott, and as a result he studied the Bible with renewed earnestness. After ardent study of the New Testament in Greek, as well as continual self-examination, Scott concluded that the teachings of his Presbyterian background were insufficient and incorrect. The messiahship of Jesus was the only true creed of the Christian faith. Scott recounted the following in his book *The Messiahship*:

> After a brief party history, sweet and refreshing was the rest experienced on reaching the great generalization of the Messiahship. Freed from the embarrassment incident to the consideration of a mass of unassorted particulars, [I] felt that [I] had reached the true beginning of the Christian religion, and was strong in this comprehensive knowledge.[20]

The true beginning of Christian religion was the confession that Jesus is the Messiah, the Son of God. Scott turned to this confession as the foundational statement of Christian belief, and turned away from the creedalism of his Scots-Presbyterian background. Soon after this "turn" occurred, Forrester tragically drowned. As a result of the death of his mentor and friend, Scott took on the

---

[18]Dwight E. Stevenson, *Walter Scott: Voice of the Golden Oracle* (Saint Louis: Christian Board of Publication, 1946), p. 24.

[19]Lester G. McAllister and William E. Tucker, *Journey in Faith: A History of the Christian Church (Disciples of Christ)* (St. Louis: CB Press, 1975), pp. 130; 97.

[20]Walter Scott, *The Messiahship or Great Demonstration Written for the Union of Christians on Christian Principles, as Plead for in the Current Reformation* (Cincinnati: H. S. Bosworth, 1859), p. 7.

full-time ministry of his primitive church. From this humble beginning the evangelist developed his message of the Golden Oracle.

Explicit Creed: The Golden Oracle

Walter Scott's thinking did not escape the influence of his time in history. The teachings of Bacon and Scottish Common Sense had a profound effect upon him. Scott's conception of the confession of Jesus as the Messiah evidences this fact. "In Scott's thinking the central theme of the Scriptures and the key to their interpretation was the messiahship of Jesus Christ. This was, for Scott, the fundamental truth of the Christian faith and the Creed of Christianity; he called it 'the Golden Oracle.'"[21] There is a connection between Scott's understanding of the Golden Oracle and his perception of the Common Sense Realism idea of a *first principle.*

Thomas Reid, one of the major figures of Scottish Common Sense Realism, described the nature of a first principle as foundational. In the analysis of a proposition or a statement of truth, one determines whether it is self-evident or if it rests upon one or more propositions that support it. He asserted that this examination can only end when one finds a proposition that supports all that is built upon it, and is itself supported by none; these are the only propositions rightly described to be self-evident.[22] For Scott, the primary self-evident proposition of Christianity was that Jesus is the Messiah, the Son of God. He states, "In the philosophical investigation of any system, after ascending to first principles, it becomes our privilege to descend from these principles to the exposition of all facts and phenomena connected with the system."[23]

Scott listed three items as first principles of Christianity: the Messiahship, the Doctrine, and the Proof.[24] Thus, for Scott, the Messiahship is one of three first principles of Christianity. Any other statements of belief are unnecessary for Christian faith, because if they do form a part of the Christian faith, "they, nevertheless, do not form its first principles."[25] The Golden Oracle is a self-evident proposition due to the fact that the confession is confirmed by the testimony of the one God. "'Behold my Son, the Beloved, in whom I delight.' As God is the author of this grand oracle, so our Lord

[21]Gerrard, "Walter Scott: Frontier Disciples Evangelist," p. 36.

[22]*The Works of Thomas Reid*, ed. Sir William Hamilton, vol. 1, *The Philosophical Works of Thomas Reid* (Edinburgh: James Thin, 1845), p. 434.

[23]Scott, *The Messiahship*, p. 271.

[24]Ibid.

[25]Walter Scott, *The Gospel Restored* (Cincinnati: Ormsby H. Donogh, 1836), p. 184.

has built his church on it; that is, he has decreed that whoever confesses it shall be admitted a member of the church."[26] This confession is no theory; it is a fact. According to Scott, "Christianity stands on a basis of reality—an organic truth—a creed—something to be believed in order to salvation."[27] The truth of the Golden Oracle is proven by the fact that God testified as to its truth. To understand this position, one must understand Scott's distinction between knowledge and faith.

For Scott, one acquires knowledge by direct sensory experience, and one acquires faith based upon the believability of the testimony of others. Adam and Eve had knowledge of God because they walked in the Garden with God and had direct sensory experience of the Deity. The apostles had knowledge due to their direct sensory experience of Jesus. All who have not had this direct experience must rest their faith on the testimony of those who have. As such, Christians are to have faith in the statement that Jesus is the Messiah, the Son of God, because the Bible records that it was God who testified on behalf of this fact. At the baptism of Jesus, the voice of God spoke and declared, "Behold my son." Scott asserted, "That Jesus is [God's] son must be a fact, or God could not have testified to it."[28] This testimony of the Almighty God as to the identity of Jesus serves as incontrovertible proof of the truth of the Golden Oracle. If one relies on testimony as the basis of faith, then the testimony of God is ultimate. This argument is necessarily linked to Scott's propositional understanding of scripture.

Scott understood scripture as a record of truths that are univocal in meaning. He perceived scripture to contain propositional truth.[29] In propositional truth, the words and the actual events have a one-to-one correlation. Scott stated, "Accordingly, the 'first truth' in the Gospel was imparted to mankind with great majesty and glory at the river Jordan, when our Lord Jesus Christ was baptized."[30] The scriptural account of the attestation of God at the baptism of Jesus was understood by Scott as a historical record. Scott defined faith as belief in the Messiahship as proved by God's attestation.[31] Faith is belief in a testimony given by an infallible

---

[26]Walter Scott, "Confession," *The Evangelist* (May 1838): p. 119.

[27]Scott, *The Union of Christians*, p. 3.

[28]Scott, *The Gospel Restored*, p. 195.

[29]Larry Bouchard, "The Interpretation Principle," in *Interpreting Disciples: Practical Theology in the Disciples of Christ*, ed. L. Dale Richesin (Fort Worth: Texas Christian University Press, 1987), p. 13.

[30]Scott, *The Union of Christians*, p. 8.

[31]Scott, *The Messiahship*, p. 271.

witness. One could argue, therefore, that the confession does not act as a first principle in strictest terms as it is attested and proved by evidence (God's testimony) and is therefore not self-evident. However, one must acknowledge as well that Scott understood the testimony of God in scripture to be propositionally true and indisputable.

The fact that it is God who testifies sets this proposition apart from those propositions proved by human testimony. The confession of Jesus as the Messiah is the primary first principle of Christianity because testimony about its truth is provided by the infallible God. As such, the Golden Oracle acted as a first principle for Scott, although in reality it did not fit neatly into the philosophical definition set out by Reid and others. Given Scott's propositional understanding of scripture and his existence in a prehistorical critical world, one can better understand his definition of the confession as a self-evident proposition, or first principle.

Scott's explanation of the importance of the confession also reflects the first principle characteristic of fundamentality. While Scott acknowledges two other items as first principles, the confession stands alone as the foundational proposition for Christianity. In further explication of first principles, Reid stated that "every conclusion got by reasoning must rest with its whole weight upon first principles, as the building does upon its foundation."[32] It is apparent that Scott saw the confession of Jesus Christ as the foundation of Christianity. Scott stated:

> There is nothing in the Christian religion more extraordinary than that its author is the Son of God, even as there is nothing more fundamental; the man, therefore, who has surely believed this, has surmounted all difficulty in regard to becoming a Christian and an heir to the privileges, honors, and promises of the institution. This oracle is, therefore, made the subject of public, and personal confession. In short, it is the creed of Christianity, original Christianity; and he who believes the fact may become a Christian.[33]

The Messiahship as a first principle is fundamental, and it is also apprehensible. A first principle is a proposition that is immediately believable and can be apprehended as soon as it is

[32]*The Works of Thomas Reid*, ed. Sir William Hamilton, vol.1, *The Philosophical Works of Thomas Reid* (Edinburgh: James Thin, 1845), p. 435.

[33]Scott, *The Gospel Restored*, p. 185.

understood. A first principle is accessible to the human mind by means of simple human logic, and such apprehension is a naturally occurring part of being human. As easily as a first principle can be explained, it can be grasped. Reid equated the ease of judging these first principles with the swallowing of food. Like swallowing, "It is purely natural and therefore common to the learned and unlearned...it requires ripeness of understanding, and freedom from prejudice, but nothing else."[34] Scott agreed, saying:

> In bestowing on man a capacity for knowledge, God bestowed on him a capacity for faith also; but faith is the principle on which all the blessings of Christianity may be received, therefore men everywhere have a capacity for receiving the blessings of Christianity; or in other words, the gospel, in its principle of faith or belief, is adapted to human nature universally.[35]

The Golden Oracle is foundational, easily accessible, and stands alone as the creed of Christianity. It is also the key to the restoration of the church.

Scott believed the restoration of the primitive New Testament church would bring about the original unity of the church and usher in the millennium. Consequently, all additions to the primitive faith were unacceptable and needed to be rejected. "Pure doctrine," reformers urged, "could be established only by confining religious discourse to the direct propositions of scripture—without any additions whatsoever 'of human authority, of private opinion, or inventions of men.'"[36] Scott understood the primitive church to be pure, describing that "her only manual was the Bible, and her creed, for the binding together of all who obeyed her, was Jesus is the Son of God."[37]

Walter Scott searched for a means to proclaim effectively this world-transforming message of the foundational import of this confession about Jesus Christ.[38] He developed a system to proclaim the Messiahship, but he also preached the necessary results of the

---

[34]Hamilton, ed., *The Works of Thomas Reid,* p. 434.

[35]Scott, *The Gospel Restored,* p. 259.

[36]Alexander Campbell, "An Oration in Honor of the Fourth of July, 1830," in *Popular Lectures and Addresses* (Philadelphia, 1863), p. 374, quoted in Allen and Hughes, *Innocence,* p. 157.

[37]Scott, *The Gospel Restored,* p. 184.

[38]Allen and Hughes, *Innocence,* p. 159.

confession as he discerned them in scripture. The Golden Oracle was not just the good confession—"Jesus is the Christ"—in isolation, but a statement entailing lengthy items of explanation as to how this affirmation *must* be understood. These items, though not explicitly set forth by Scott in order to avoid "the confession of a plurality of matters,"[39] were still the basic and essential assertions of his belief system. They make up his implicit creed.

Implicit Creed

All Scott deemed necessary for salvation was the belief in Jesus as the Messiah and the confession of that belief. This is the one belief required of Christians. However, he understood this confession to produce obedient actions in response. He stated:

> It is a logical consequence, therefore, from all the premises before us, that if we would meet the conditions of salvation, we must accept the Gospel—believe it. We must make the belief of it a reality, by confessing Christ, by reforming our life, and obeying the Gospel; for if a man receive it, he must receive it with its practical designs.[40]

The "practical designs" of belief in Jesus Christ make up Scott's implicit creed. Whereas the believer has been commanded to believe by God's statement "Behold my Son," the believer is commanded to obedience by God's assertion, "Hear you him."[41] The confessed believer is to hear the words of Jesus as recorded in scripture and is to obey his commands. Scott described the order of the response to confession. He portrayed it as the move from what we should *know* to what we should *do*, from what God has revealed to what God has commanded, from what God has done to what God has commanded us to do for ourselves.[42] For Scott, the duties following confession include repentance and baptism. Obedient completion of these duties brings about God's fulfillment of the promises made in scripture. These promises are the remission of sins, the gift of the Holy Spirit, and eternal life. Scott called these items first principles,[43] but did not claim they were self-evident. They are dependent upon the confession of the Messiahship of

---

[39]Ibid.
[40]Scott, *The Union of Christians*, p. 80.
[41]Scott, *The Gospel Restored*, p. 225.
[42]Ibid.
[43]Scott, *The Messiahship*, p. 293.

Jesus. They do not describe the faith, or what is to be believed, but what is to be done. They are prescriptive of the believer's action.

Scott explained, "Principles are invisible; we do not ask what they are, but what they do. Faith is a principle; and therefore, without perplexing ourselves with the question, What is faith? I prefer asking for the sake of the answer. 'What does faith?'"[44] Scott then provided the answer to his own questions, stating that faith results in repentance and obedience. Repentance and obedience result in the privileges of Christianity, including the remission of sins, the gift of the Holy Spirit, and eternal life. This formula of what will necessarily come to pass following the confession of Jesus as Messiah served as a kind of creed for Scott. Scott's implicit creed acts not so much as a further explication of right belief, but as an assertion of right action in response to right belief, and the reward given by God in response to right action.[45] Right action for Scott first required right apprehension; the penitent must be able to understand the message proclaimed. Scott espoused a reasonable, rational, logical faith.

Scott does not specifically list a reasonable faith as one of the duties or privileges of Christian faith. He did, however, state:

> It is not to be denied that Christianity demands faith; but then, it is equally certain that it proposes facts for our faith. Had it called for faith irrespective of facts, or for faith in facts, irrespective of evidence, then Christianity and reason would have been [opposites]; but these things it does *not* do. In Christianity there is a proposition, and there is a proof; there are facts, and there is evidence; and this is the reason why it both demands and commands belief.[46]

While Scott expected much of the confessed believer, he did not expect belief to come without evidence. As such, it is essential to examine Scott's belief in a reasonable faith and to understand it

---

[44]Scott, *The Union of Christians*, p. 76.

[45]Larry Bouchard, "The Interpretation Principle," *Interpreting Disciples*, p. 16. Bouchard defines theology as "the concerned and thoughtful inquiry into the foundations of faith, the meaning of beliefs, and the implications of both for human experience and action in the world." He continues by affirming that Disciples have a "foundational theology," which is "thought about the very bases of Christian faith and thought." He asserts that theology is activity. As such, Walter Scott fits into this conception of a foundational theology in his emphasis on basic Christian themes such as Jesus Christ and the Bible, as well as his stress upon Christian life as activity in response to God.

[46]Scott, *The Evangelist* (April 1839): p. 4.

as a primary component in his implicit creed. Although he called for dutiful response, this call came only after the conviction of the truth of the gospel evidence. Scott preached a message he assumed to be apprehensible by human reasoning. He preached with this assumption and taught with this as a part of his worldview. As such, reasonable faith is the first item in Scott's implicit creed.

Reasonable Faith

In 1827, Walter Scott declared that the gospel was restored.[47] Scott quoted the report in the religious journal *The Millennial Harbinger*, which read:

> Brother Walter Scott arranged the several items of faith, repentance, baptism, remission of sins, the Holy Spirit, and eternal life, restored them in this order to the church, under the title of ancient gospel, and preached it successfully to the world.[48]

Scott's excitement about his arrangement of the gospel rested in part in his confidence in the human ability to understand it. Scott realized that "It is of the essence of the human mind to infer truth from proof."[49] He asserted, "Faith is the *evidence* or confidence of things not seen. The word in the Greek, which stands for *evidence,* denotes a *strict proof* or *demonstration*. A proof which thoroughly convinces understanding, and determines the will."[50] The Gospel, if presented properly, could not fail to stir the heart and mind of the hearer. In his restored plan of the gospel, Scott felt he had achieved a system that could act as powerful proof of the truth of Christianity.

The acceptance of the gospel required a rational endorsement of the evidence of scripture. "In bestowing on man a capacity for knowledge, God bestowed on him a capacity for faith."[51] Scott's system was predicated on a crucial order he discerned as present in the Bible. One must be rationally persuaded of the truth of scripture *before* one confesses Jesus as the Messiah. "'If thou confess with thy mouth the Lord Jesus, and believe in thy heart that God raised him from the dead, thou shalt be saved.' It is not demanded, however, that a man shall confess before he believes, or that he

---

[47]Scott, *The Gospel Restored,* p. v.

[48]Ibid., p. vi.

[49]Scott, *The Messiahship*, p. 272.

[50]Scott, "The Nature, and Causes of Faith, Considered," *The Evangelist* (August 1833): p. 183.

[51]Scott, *The Gospel Restored*, p. 259.

shall believe before he has examined. This [is] absurd."[52] The rational explication of scripture must convince the penitent of the believability of the scriptural witness, or there will be no confession of Jesus as the Messiah in the first place. Rational understanding is the prerequisite to confession. To confess truly with one's heart, one must also be convicted in one's mind. Garrison added:

> [Scott's message] assumed both the rationality of man and his moral ability to take the first step toward his own salvation. That first step was to examine the evidence, and so, by the use of his own intellect, to arrive at a reasoned faith in the messiahship of Jesus. There was something to believe and there were reasons for believing it. There was something to do that you could do. And there were definite promises conditioned upon belief and obedience.[53]

In this, Scott responded in part to the beliefs prevalent in the revivals occurring on the frontier at that time. Although the understanding that belief came before confession was important in itself for Scott, it became increasingly more so in the face of the camp meetings.

In camp meetings of this time "the revivalist's only duty was to instruct sinners in the truth of the gospel and to urge them to repent and pray in the hope that God had predestined them for salvation."[54] God's predestination could only be revealed by the work of the Holy Spirit. The Spirit created an emotional response within the penitent that acted as a sign that his or her sins were remitted. Based upon this proof, sinners could then be baptized and receive salvation. Many waited for extended periods of time, laying across anxious benches, hoping for the conviction of the Spirit.

Scott found this process inane. "Instead of planting the faith of the Gospel on an infallible demonstration, the Lord's resurrection, etc., the hypothesis plants it on the shifting sands of frames and feelings, and seeks to make men feel rather than believe."[55] Scott stood in vehement opposition to any idea that humanity could not respond of its own will, but must wait for a mysterious action of the Holy Spirit. This rational emphasis of Scott's led to a different understanding of the process of salvation.

---

[52]Scott, *The Evangelist* (April 1839): p. 74.
[53]Garrison, *Religion Follows the Frontier*, pp. 125–126.
[54]McLoughlin, *Modern Revivalism*, p. 32.
[55]Scott, *The Union of Christians*, p. 78.

The order often referred to as Scott's "five-finger exercise" set out in simple language the path to salvation. One confesses, repents, and is baptized. Following baptism, one receives the remission of sins and is given the gift of the Holy Spirit and eternal life. This order represented a change from the progression taught by many other groups, influenced by Calvinism and predestination, operating in the frontier setting. For Scott, the Bible alone contained the necessary proof required for the conviction of the hearer. The creed of Jesus the Messiah, preached and rationally accepted, "rescues us from the dominion of the senses and clears away from the mind all false centers, both of faith and affection, and places both on Christ."[56] One is convinced of the Messiahship of Jesus by hearing the word proclaimed. This propositional truth then informs and clarifies all other knowledge of scripture. It is the fundamental oracle to be believed and upon its acceptance all else will fall smoothly into place.

This conception of the path to salvation attracted the frontier people for many reasons. Its popularity resulted from its appeal to the rational abilities of the human mind and the respect for the capacity of human beings to make decisions. Scott's message appealed to those who had not been able to relate to the emotional experience of salvation required by other groups on the frontier, and to those who had become frustrated or confused by doctrinal requirements. Scott's process was simple. The believer, moved by the rational discourse of scripture, is struck by his or her unworthiness, led to repent of sinful ways, and compelled to come forward for baptism for the remission of those sins. This baptism for the remission of sins represents the next element contained within Scott's implicit creed.

Baptism: Christian Duty

If the confession of Jesus as the Messiah was Scott's organic principle, then baptism was the organic ordinance or action, directly predicated upon the statement of belief.[57] He developed this understanding over a period of many years. In the spring of 1821, Scott gained access to a pamphlet entitled "On Baptism," published by a congregation in New York that adhered to many current Haldane beliefs.[58] It had a profound effect on his life and teaching.

---

[56]Scott, *The Messiahship*, p. 273.
[57]Scott, *The Union of Christians*, p. 89.
[58]Baxter, *The Life of Elder Walter Scott*, p. 46.

Within its pages, he discovered a startling new approach to the practice of baptism. Amazed and delighted, he read and realized that "baptism was more than a symbol or ordinance. It was a positive Christian action! Scott found himself startled into agreement that it was 'in baptism that men professed by deed, as they had already done by word, to have the remission of sins through the death of Jesus Christ.'"[59]

Inspired by this teaching, Scott began to reformulate his understanding of baptism as he saw it revealed in scripture. He asserted, "The kingdom of God, its privileges and blessings are conditioned by duty. It is duty first and privilege afterward. Duties: 1. Faith. 2. Repentance. 3. Baptism. Privileges: 1. Remission of sins. 2. The Holy Spirit. 3. Eternal life."[60] Once one is convicted by reason to confess, and upon that conviction repents of sin, the next step is to follow the instructions of the Christ. "Arise; 'why tarriest thou, arise and be baptized and wash away thy sins, calling upon the name of the Lord.'"[61]

Based on his own intensive study of baptism and its practice in the Bible, Scott saw baptism as the means by which sins are forgiven. The words of Acts 2:38 were clear as to the charge assigned to those who would be Christians: "Then Peter said unto them, Repent, and be baptized every one of you in the name of Jesus Christ for the remission of sins, and ye shall receive the gift of the Holy Ghost."[62] According to Scott, the remission of sin was possible only after confession, repentance, and baptism, and not before, because people could become candidates for baptism only through the rational acceptance of the evidence of scripture.[63] Scott regarded the obedient act of baptism following confession and repentance as a demand of the confessed Christ upon the believer. In a dialogue found in *The Evangelist*, Scott made the following responses:

> *Question:* Have persons baptized but who neither repent nor believe, received the remission of their sins? *Answer:* You have nothing to do with such a question. Mind what

[59]Dwight E. Stevenson, *Walter Scott, Voice of the Golden Oracle* (St. Louis: Christian Board of Publication, 1946), pp. 28–29.

[60]Scott, *The Messiahship*, p. 293.

[61]Scott, *The Gospel Restored*, p. 194.

[62]Acts 2:38 (*New Revised Standard Version*).

[63]L. Edward Hicks, "Rational Religion in the Ohio Western Reserve (1827–1830): Walter Scott and the Restoration Appeal of Baptism for the Remission of Sins," *Restoration Quarterly* 34, no. 4 (1992): p. 217.

> the Son of God has said, and the Apostles have taught and practiced; forgiveness is consequent on faith, repentance, and baptism; but you ask. *Question:* Are these merely *expected* of him who is a candidate for pardon? *Answer:* This is a silly impertinent question: these things are not only expected but demanded of every candidate for pardon.[64]

Baptism was not a magical act, but was the dutiful response of the faith of the believer, and that faith's great desire to do all Christ commanded. This dutiful obedience is what brings about the remission of sin. Scott did acknowledge, however, the possibility that one could feel forgiven without being baptized. The apprehension of the gospel could indeed bring about a change in one's life, even without baptism. He had seen too much of this very thing at camp meetings to deny it. This change, however, was not a change of state. Baptism was necessary for a change of that magnitude. The people who experienced the emotional benefits of confession but were not baptized had not received the change of state from sinfulness to pardon and justification. According to Scott, "they have not received an acquittal from their former sins in the way and by the ordinance of baptism, which the great head of the church has appointed for the forgiveness of sins."[65] People who have not been baptized might feel forgiven, but they are not; not until they have been immersed. Scott's views on baptism stood in opposition to many other prevalent understandings in American Protestantism.

The Baptists understood that baptism took place *after* sins are forgiven; Scott would have nothing of that theology. In addition, Scott responded strongly to the practice of infant baptism found in other Protestant traditions. He asserted:

> Who are to be baptized, or immersed, one who believes, or one who does not believe? There is not one word [in scripture] enjoining it on any person to baptize his children. The command is not baptize your children, but be yourself baptized for the remission of your sins.[66]

Children are unable to apprehend the Bible rationally, to be convicted by their truth, and repent of their sins. As such, they cannot be baptized, because baptism is for the remission of sins

[64]Scott, "Baptism," *The Evangelist* (April 1834): p. 83.
[65]Scott, *The Gospel Restored*, p. 296.
[66]Ibid.

and is predicated upon the conviction that Jesus is the Messiah. Such a conviction is only available to the fully–developed rational human mind. This is in addition to the fact that there was no scriptural referent to support the practice. Scott here also equates baptism with immersion, another conviction that arose out of his study of scripture.

Scott first publicly espoused this belief concerning the remission of sin through immersion in New Lisbon, Ohio, in November of 1827 when he declared the gospel restored. The basic concept of baptism for the remission of sins had been discussed by Campbell earlier, but Scott, as usual, found the most effective way to represent it to the people. On this occasion in Ohio, "[Scott] believed that for the first time in modern times the preaching of 'the Gospel restored' included baptism for the remission of sin. The hinge on which the acceptance of the gospel swung was the element of baptism."[67] Baptism was the transitional moment for the believer, the avenue of entrance into the church. It was the "culminating act of the penitent believer in obedience to Christ and the turning of the soul to God."[68] In baptism, the faith expressed by the believer is made apparent, and for Scott, this was a faith in the atoning blood of Jesus Christ.

Baptism was indeed a baptism into the life, death, and resurrection of the Christ, and in this action, the confessing Christian is assured of God's forgiveness and mercy. Scott contended, "we are forgiven not because we are baptized, but because we need forgiveness, and are by faith prepared to receive it through the merits of Christ alone."[69] Faith must be allowed to "perform its internal and external work on [one] before [one] is fitted for pardon."[70] Accordingly, it is not just to characterize Scott as inordinately dependent upon his high estimate of human reason, as he acknowledged in baptism the ultimate act of God in the remission of sins. Although the confessing believer could institute the process, the final act was God's through Christ. By this action of God in baptism, the transformation of the state of the believer occurs, and the work of the Spirit is now available.[71]

Baptism was the pivot point in Scott's theology from the actions of the believer to the actions of God. It is within baptism that

---

[67]Hicks, "Rational Religion," p. 218.

[68]Gerrard, "Walter Scott: Frontier Disciples Evangelist," p. 138.

[69]Scott, *The Gospel Restored*, p. 299.

[70]Ibid., p. 301.

[71]Gerrard, "Walter Scott: Frontier Disciples Evangelist," p. 246.

the believer encounters the Holy Spirit, and it was the last of the duties Scott saw as essential for the confessing believer to accomplish. Scott stated, "Now, we are commanded to be baptized, in order that we may also receive the Holy Spirit."[72] The shift has occurred, and it is time for the believer to experience the "privileges" of Christianity, the primary one being the advent of the Holy Spirit, the third and final element within Scott's implicit creed.

Conceptualization of the Holy Spirit

Scott believed that the believer received the Holy Spirit only after the accomplishment of the steps of confession, repentance, and baptism. "Now, therefore, the baptized convert...is an heir of the promise of the Holy Spirit first. He has been washed and justified in the name of the Lord Jesus Christ, and is now to be 'sanctified by the Spirit of our God.'"[73] As simple a progression as this seems, it directly opposed the understanding of the activity of the Holy Spirit prominent in the churches influenced and directed by Calvinism. This is the same Calvinist teaching Scott opposed on the grounds of his belief in a rational faith. There are, however, some nuances to be explored regarding the activity of the Holy Spirit.

Scott repudiated the idea of regenerating or enabling grace, a concept of the Spirit linked to an understanding of human nature as irredeemable and corrupt. According to this belief, humanity cannot take the first necessary steps toward salvation due to its depravity caused by original sin. Thus, the seeker after God must wait until there is a direct action of the Holy Spirit which enables conversion and regeneration.[74] Many Calvinists measured a person's piety by the number of months spent "agonizing" before finding salvation.[75] A jingle popular at this time "summed up the frustrating and apparently contradictory tenets of Calvinism regarding [humanity's] part in conversion":

> You can and you can't.
> You will and you won't.
> You're damned if you do,
> And damned if you don't.[76]

---

[72]Scott, *The Union of Christians*, p. 24.
[73]Ibid., p. 108.
[74]Gerrard, "Walter Scott: Frontier Disciples Evangelist," p. 246.
[75]McLoughlin, *Modern Revivalism*, p. 98.
[76]Ibid., p. 21.

Scott considered this conceptualization of faith anathema. This is not surprising considering his profound belief in humanity's ability to take the needed steps to begin the journey toward salvation. In a dialogue he created between himself and a questioner, the questioner asked Scott in amazement, "You mean me then to seek this great good by obeying the Gospel, and go to Jesus Christ with all my feebleness, fears, and transgressions about me?" And Scott answered, "Yes."[77] This yes stood as a firm "no" to the teachings of the Calvin-based revivals and churches.

For Scott, "The Holy Spirit is a blessing given and bestowed on the obedient after baptism, but never before faith."[78] One is led toward God through the reception of the Word of God in scripture. Once convinced of the reasonableness of the evidence presented for belief, one confesses and repents, and is baptized. There is no need in this construction for the "enabling grace" of the Holy Spirit. The Spirit acts until the point of baptism as the means of inspiration of the Bible. Scott contended, "Is it nowhere said in Scripture, that the Spirit must convince us of sin? Yes; but we have already seen how he does this: namely, by the word of God, preached—not by going into the souls of sinners."[79] The inspirational effect of the scripture will lead people to confess, not some mystical movement of the Spirit.

"By teaching that regeneration is that change which is called conversion, and that the Holy Spirit affects this by an undeniable influence on the sinner's mind, we render the Word of God of none effect. We make it a dead letter, and absolutely blaspheme it."[80] For Scott, such blaspheming of the scripture was the same as blasphemy of the Holy Spirit, the unforgivable sin. "What then, is to be the fate of that man, who sins against the Holy Spirit, and by refusing [the Spirit's] testimony in this important matter, sets aside the great fact of the Messiahship on which the redemption of man is founded?"[81] The answer is the loss of the chance for salvation. The desire for salvation was profoundly important to the people who came to hear Scott preach.

Garrison echoed what must have been the convert's feelings, stating:

---

[77]Scott, *The Gospel Restored*, p. 412.

[78]Scott, *The Messiahship*, p. 294.

[79]Gerrard, "Walter Scott : Frontier Disciples Evangelist," p. 92.

[80]Scott, *The Gospel Restored*, p. 453.

[81]Ibid., p. 211.

> When the convert had believed, repented, and obeyed, he could be perfectly sure that he was saved. He had the promise of God for it. No need to mourn and agonize and wait for some special act of enabling grace or some emotional experience which would be a guaranty of his acceptance with God.[82]

This account of one of Scott's evangelistic visits offers a revealing comment on Scott's method of baptism and his understanding of the Holy Spirit. It is recorded that Scott received converts for baptism "on the confession of their faith in the Lord Jesus Christ, without the usual routine of telling an 'experience.'"[83] By not requiring the confession of an experience of the Holy Spirit, Scott plainly asserted that the convert had come to this state of faith, repentance, and conversion through the confession of Jesus as Messiah. This is a confession arrived at through reason and by demonstration, and not by the direct and unavoidable influence of the Holy Spirit.

With the gift of the Spirit, Scott's formula was complete. The one who confessed, repented, and was baptized, gained remission of sins and received the Holy Spirit, and could now "stand on a footing with all saints and become a partaker of the blessings and graces of God's spirit."[84] These graces included the blessing of eternal life. Salvation, by means described by this implicit creed, was achieved.

Conclusion

For Walter Scott, the gospel restored was the gospel presented in a logical formulation easily understood by the common person. With this foundational understanding of the gospel, his preaching and teaching took a structure and form that could be effectively communicated. To Scott's way of thinking, his successes were more than simply evangelical triumphs. His message was more than a means by which to beat out competition for church membership. The gospel restored was the means by which the world would be transformed.

Scott fully expected the restoration of the gospel to bring about

---

[82]Garrison, *Religion Follows the Frontier*, p. 126.

[83]A. S. Hayden, *Early History of the Disciples in the Western Reserve, Ohio* (Presbyterian Theological Seminary; Cincinnati: Chase and Hall Publishers, 1875, textfiche), p. 117, 1988–0745.

[84]Scott, "Of the True Gospel," *The Evangelist* (December 1842): p. 275.

the restoration of the primitive church, the renewal of the original unity of Christianity, the advent of the millennium and the triumph of Christianity in all the world. The creed of Jesus Christ and its implicit structure of right belief and response was the means by which the world could be saved. This structure was predicated upon the first principle of Jesus as the Messiah, the Son of God. In addition, the structure included the necessary accompaniments to that confession: repentance, baptism for the remission of sins, the gift of the Holy Spirit, and the realization of the promise of eternal life. Scott was devoted to this ideal of a simple and God-given faith, a faith without the "trappings" of human constructions.

It seems, however, to be the fate of most faith systems that they must find some construction, some means of being intelligible and accessible. In theory, Scott would claim these means to be already present in the Bible, and, in fact, within the simple confession that Jesus is the Messiah. Apparently, such a simple confession was not enough even for Scott who claimed its sufficiency. The result of this necessary construction of a faith system, and its popularity in the evangelistic efforts of the reform movement, was a people who proclaimed no need for human creeds. These same people, however, were inspired to follow the masterful system of faith of one very *human* being, Walter Scott.

In an article he wrote for the journal *The Evangelist*, Scott speaks of the practices of night fishing. In an attempt to draw the fish to the surface, the fishermen would hold out a flame or flambeau, as Scott calls it.[85] Scott equated the lure of the "flambeau" and its ability to attract the fish with the power of the gospel to attract people. Just as the fish are drawn by the light and the activity of the flame, people are drawn to the word of God. It is my belief that the flame held out by Scott was carefully and lovingly constructed so as to be the most efficient and effective flame possible, with a light that was easy to see and a comfort to draw near. It was a flame burning with the conviction that what was offered was not only personal salvation, but the salvation of all the world. Walter Scott, the fiery preacher of the Reformers, held out his system of belief to all who came searching. This offering was his powerful gift to his movement, his devoted attempt to serve God, his best presentation of his beloved faith, and his creed.

---

[85]Scott, "Faith," *The Evangelist* (April 1832): p. 86.

CHAPTER THREE

Walter Scott, Theologian

James O. Duke

My title "Walter Scott, Theologian" may seem at first glance outlandish to anyone familiar with the lore of the Stone-Campbell movement. Theologian-baiting was perhaps the only blood sport the movement condoned. Scott never called himself a theologian. While he lived not even his enemies, much less his friends, claimed he should have. Thereafter, most of the few people who know of him at all know the legendary Scott, and legend has it Scott was no theologian. True, he was born and bred Scots Presbyterian, and Edinburgh trained at the height of the Scots Renaissance. But his fame was due to his resolve to overcome handicaps such as these. He became an evangelist instead of a theologian, and a soul-winning success, because he cared not a whit about theology and asked would-be Christians only to go and do likewise. He liked the Bible, alone; the gospel, ancient and simple; the church, restored to its ancient, apostolic, pretheological perfection.

The legendary Scott still lives in the corporate memory of his heirs, denominational or undenominational, who are now dispersed as the Christian Church (Disciples of Christ), the Churches of Christ, and the Christian Churches. Little, except Scott's writings, extracts of stump sermons included, casts doubt on it. It is not impossible to find there glimpses of Scott, the theology-free ideal. Yet they are all too few and fleeting. His works, much like those of the two Campbells and Stone, produce in readers today that certain (as it were very special, sinking) feeling that comes with the realization that early leaders of the nineteenth-century Reformation were, notwithstanding their disclaimers, trafficking in theology on America's trans-Appalachian frontier.

Scott's literary output was formidable. There is *A Discourse on the Holy Spirit*, 24 pages; *The Gospel Restored*, 576 pages; *To Themelion, or, The Union of Christians*, 128 pages; *He Nekrosis, or the Death of Christ*, 132 pages; *The Messiahship*, 384 pages. Most of the materials in over fifteen annual journal volumes, except in latter years, were written by Scott's hand, as were over twenty articles in other journals.[1] In search of a likely nontheological topic, one might turn to his Bacon College presidential address on "The State System (and the Elements of Universal Education, National Education, the Education of the United States, and the National Character)." Yet roughly one third of its forty-seven pages are devoted to an exposition of a new edition of the *Novum Organum* (1619) by Sir Francis Bacon, Lord Verulam, celebrated founder of "Experimental Philosophy."[2]

Surveying this mass of writings, readers are unlikely to find that any of them are so strictly biblical, divinely simple, eminently practical, and utterly oblivious to any theological tradition that whatever it may be, it is anything but theology. In fact, Scott seems to be a Christian with a faith-seeking understanding. He seems to be a teacher of the church's faith, indeed a teacher of the church's teachers. He seems an invariably serious-minded, typically studious, and frequently scholarly inquirer into the nature, meaning, and validity of the Christian message. In sum, Scott seems like someone that everybody in the whole wide world would readily take for a Christian theologian, unless and until members of the Stone-Campbell movement advised them otherwise.

My aim here is merely to read his works like any others, as historians of the church and its theology usually do. Hence, to call them theology and him a theologian is neither a mistake nor a slur.

---

[1]For a recent listing of Scott's writings, see the bibliographies in William Austin Gerrard III, "Walter Scott: Frontier Disciples Evangelist," (Ph.D. diss., Emory University; Ann Arbor, Mich: University Microfilms, 1982) ; revised as *A Biographical Study of Walter Scott: American Frontier Evangelist* (Joplin, Mo.: College Press Publishing Co., 1992).

[2]Walter Scott, "The State System," *The Christian* (February and March 1837): pp. 25–72; reprint: "United States System: An Address," *The College of the Bible Quarterly* (April 1946): pp. 4–44.

The point at issue turns mainly on gaining what Alexander Campbell termed the proper "understanding distance" on the texts at hand, that is, giving due regard to what today might be called contextualization. This is never an easy task, and Scott is hardly as helpful as one would wish.

One obstacle is that he uses the word theology only occasionally and equivocally, and gives mixed signals about his attitude toward it. Along with his barbs at the creedifiers, "theologists" [*sic*], and philosophers come a few kind words for true theology. He maintained, for example, that in the days of Caesar Augustus "the true Theology" had become a necessity the great teacher, Lord Jesus Christ, then supplied, and that all will be held responsible on the day of judgment to give account for their faithfulness to the Savior's teachings regarding character, morality, and theology.[3] In Scott's view, "the Messiahship and Divinity of Lord Jesus" is Christianity's creed,[4] and the church should require none other of those seeking membership and fellowship in the church. Yet he himself also confessed, "I believe that in Christ dwelleth all the fullness of the Godhead," while promptly disavowing any "idea of a speculative union in the Godhead."[5] He elsewhere stated God's "Trinity in unity is the true theology."[6]

He insisted it was important to adduce reasonably credible evidences that Christianity, the Bible, and the messiahship of Jesus are truly revelations of God, on one occasion urging his readers to read Lord Brougham's *A Discourse on Natural Theology* and on another urging them to devote church school classes to arguments set forth in evidentiary literature such as William Paley's *Hora*

---

[3]Walter Scott, *The Messiahship or Great Demonstration, Written for the Union of Christians, on Christian Principles, as Plead for in the Current Reformation* (Cincinnati: H. S. Bosworth, 1859), p. 262.

[4]Walter Scott, *The Union of Christians* (improved ed.: *The Union of Christians and Death of Christ*, 2 vols. in 1 (Philadelphia: James Challen and Son, 1864): 1:3.

[5]Ibid., 1:97. The passage runs: "Now, I believe that in Christ dwelleth all the fullness of the Godhead bodily—that I do this is admitted; but that no idea of a speculative union in the Godhead is indicated in the baptismal ceremony but a practical concurrence of the Father, Son, and Holy Spirit, in founding on the Divinity of Christ our great and glorious kingdom, is the fact and the doctrine meant, I am as solemnly and thoroughly convicted." Later in this book Scott affirms the trinity (p. 43) and the two natures of Christ (p. 58) but again refuses to "speculate" on the mode of union involved within the Godhead and within the person of Christ.

[6]Scott, *Messiahship*, p. 283.

Paulinae.[7] He relied on a grammatico-historical method of biblical interpretation ("inductive hermeneutics") to confirm that the koine Greek terms for baptism meant immersion, and he explicated the design, i.e., the theological meaning, of baptism by immersion for the remission of sins in terms of a Lockean distinction between primary and secondary qualities.[8] He spoke of the four Gospels as Christianity's "logics," the New Testament epistles as its "dialectics."[9] He called the Bible verse "Behold my Son, the Beloved in whom I delight" not only "the divine oracle" but "the great generalization."[10]

Another obstacle is his conflicted attitude toward his home church and his own post-Reformation Protestant roots. Concerned to defend biblical Christianity against those he viewed as its opponents (e.g., atheists, skeptics, infidels, fanatics, and Roman Catholics), he allied himself with Protestants at large and moderates of the English and Scots Enlightenment in particular. As a champion of the movement for the recovery of the church from the sects, however, he distinguished his cause from that of his erstwhile Protestant allies, factious sectarians all. An ardent millennialist (inconstant regarding pre- and post–millennial options), he tried to explain the secrets of biblical prophecy as though his audience knew not only Daniel, John's Apocalypse, and the literature of William Miller and the "Millerites," but Herman Witsius, Campegius Vitringa, Joseph Mede, both Newtons—Sir Isaac and Bishop Thomas—and scores of other scholars as well.[11]

---

[7]On Henry, Lord Brougham, see Walter Scott, *The Gospel Restored*: A *Discourse of the True Gospel of Jesus Christ, etc.* (Cincinnati: Printed by O. H. Donogh, 1836; reprint ed. Joplin, Mo.: College Press Publishing Company, 1986), pp. 60–66; on Paley, Walter Scott, "Evidences of the Christian Religion," *Millennial Harbinger* (July 1845): p. 302, as well as "The Net: A Discourse of the Gospel," *The Evangelist* (1 January 1839): pp. 5–18.

[8]Scott, *Messiahship* pp. 284–288.

[9]Ibid., p. 25.

[10]Scott, *Gospel Restored*, p. 133; *Messiahship*, p. 7. Reference to Scott's use of the term "the golden oracle," popularized by Dwight E. Stevenson, his second biographer (*Walter Scott, Voice of the Golden Oracle: A Biography* [St. Louis: Christian Board of Publication, 1946], seems derived from reminiscences of his first, William Baxter, *Life of Elder Walter Scott* [Cincinnati: Bosworth, Chase & Hall, Pulishers, 1874]).

[11]Though Scott read widely in the scholarly and popular literature on biblical prophecy and millennialism, his passing references to authors, titles, and even passages of books are not solid proof of extensive hands-on research: one shortcut, e.g., was use of Joseph Lomas Towers, *Illustrations of Prophecy*: *In the Course of which are elucidated many predictions, which occur in Isaiah, or Daniel, in the Writings of the Evangelists... Together with a large collection of Extracts, Interspersed through the work, and taken from Numerous Commentators; and particular from Joseph Mede, Vitringa, Dr. Thomas Goodwin, Dr. Henry More, Dr. John Owen, Dr. Cressener, Peter Jurien, Brenius, Bishop Chandler, Sir Isaac Newton, Mr. William Lowth, Fleming, Bengelius, Daubuz, Whitby, Lowman, Bishop Newton, and Bishop Hurd* (2 vols., London, 1796).

The result is admittedly a very peculiar Scots-American blend. While many of its ingredients are readily tagged, there is no fully apt historical-theological label at hand for the combination as a whole. The least apt is nontheological. Scott rehearsed the grand themes and vexing conflicts of theology's opera, and did so convinced that these were matters of life and death decisions for Christians, preachers and laity alike. His aim was to grasp and then restate unvarnished biblical content, and he did his utmost to stick with the very words of *sola scriptura* (scripture alone). Even so, his efforts were, like those of theologians before and since, shaped by working now with, now through, and now against resources and options available to him.

He was caught up, often headlong, in the swirling crosscurrents of early nineteenth-century Anglo-American Protestant thought. One such current was a distinctly traditional, and at root theological, aversion to all theological tradition. Protestant–Roman Catholic polemics had led many devotees of *sola scriptura* to define biblical as "not tradition." Another was a Lockean paradigm of the referential bond of words, thoughts, and things, which Disciples considered enlightened opinion justifying their slogan "Bible words for Bible things" and led them to claim that the Bible, absent the word theology, contained none. Beyond this, however, even the most naive, nasty, and otherwise deplorable features of his thought (which were legion) were widely shared by theologians of his day.

My thesis, then, touches upon a matter of some delicacy. Hence I will deal here with only a few thin slices of his thought, and gingerly. The deceptive simplicity of his account of the ancient gospel is a case in point: first faith, repentance, and baptism (by immersion), and then remission of sins, gifts of the Holy Spirit, and eternal life.[12] What could be more simple, especially if faith is taken to mean assent to only a single proposition, that Jesus the Messiah was God's Son? Surely this is a belief one can accept or reject with little if any thought at all, afore or aft. Hordes of Scott's converts doubtless did just that, saved from thinking, if not from sinning.

Yet even the unchurched on America's nineteenth-century western frontier were more likely than Christians of later times to grasp that Scott's message was a theological response to much disputed theological issues. His audiences were diverse, not often well-schooled, some unlettered. They were by no means necessarily unintelligent. Plus, the vast majority of them had had close

---

[12]Scott organized the *Messiahship* along these lines, devoting a lengthy action to the biblical-theological meaning of each element of the *ordo*.

encounters with the basic teachings of Bible-believing Protestant Christianity. Scott's six-point schema—as legend goes, reduced to a five-finger count for publicity purposes—was a formula for what was called, by the very scholastic theologians Scott repudiated, the *ordo salutis* (the order of salvation), an ordering of the causes and effects by which the salvation of sinners is accomplished. The itemization of its elements varied in the systems and treatises of old Protestant orthodoxy. Yet few in Scott's audiences needed to know the Latin term or the scholastic textbooks in which it appeared in order to recognize that a theological message was being advanced.

Indeed, to those audiences, and to historical theologians then and thereafter, Scott's version of the *ordo salutis* was, first and foremost, another version of it. Assurance that his version was biblical, and indeed strictly, purely, and simply so, was surely welcome. This was, after all, what every *ordo salutis* was supposed to be, if it were truly Christian, truly Protestant, and truly theological. It should then come as no surprise that Scott, reared Scots Presbyterian and turning Scots Baptist before consorting with the Campbellite reform, would attend, above all else, to a "head of doctrine," and a commonplace of scholastic theology. Only his own surprise is surprising: there it was, the ancient gospel, in the Bible all along but missed until 1827 in northwestern Ohio.

What was new, of course, was not reference to the *ordo salutis* but this particular formulation of it. It came to Scott as a godsend. Indeed, unlike so many other evangelism specialists before and after him, Walter Scott could not "win" a single soul without first gaining intellectual, viz., theological, clarity about Christianity's distinctive *ordo salutis*. The inventiveness of his version of the *ordo* stamps him a theologian. Insistence that his *ordo* was neither his nor inventive, but sheerly biblical, is a telltale sign that this "simple gospel" was of mixed Swiss Reformed ancestry, via Scotland of course; while Catholics, Lutherans, and the Anglican establishment might content themselves with an *ordo salutis* that was merely not contrary to law and gospel, Scott sought one in strict accord with apostolic precept and precedent.

Another telltale sign is the fact that his *ordo* was covenant theology, and indeed a patently conditional covenant theology. This makes Scott a federal theologian (from *foedus* meaning covenant). The theme itself is eminently biblical, although scholars today are aware of ancient Near Eastern treatymaking in the background. The relation between God and humanity in history is imaged as a formal accord between two parties, involving reciprocal obligations sealed by ceremonial oaths and other sureties. At root are pledges of mutual faithfulness between God and people, who become by dint of covenant alone, become *a* people—*the* people of God.

Acknowledging God's initiative, theological accounts of covenant-making in Reformed churches followed a stereotypic pattern reducible to a brief conditional statement: God says, "I am God, and I will be your God if you will be my people." The Westminster Confession of Scott's home church is federal theology, and worth mention here, because the confessional standards of most Congregationalists and Particular ("Calvinist") Baptists, as well as the lot of Presbyterians in Scott's day were beholden to it. Westminster speaks of a double covenant, a covenant of works with Adam and a covenant of grace in Christ: the first, a promise of life conditional upon perfect obedience to God's command; the second, promise of life in Jesus Christ, "requiring of them faith in him that they may be saved."[13] The covenant conditions in both cases are set by God, and are, as such are, unilateral attestations of divine sovereignty. But the covenants themselves are bilateral, that is, mutual avowals of commitment. Bilaterality has a warm, fuzzy feel to it. But its deep logic has bite. God promises nothing to those unwilling to promise their all in return, and those who break their promises to God do so duly warned of the results.

From the mid-sixteenth century to the days of Scott (and well beyond), the covenantal motif was a staple of much Protestant church teaching, subject to endless variation. A full investigation of Scott's federalism is the stuff doctoral dissertations are made of. Here only two points—place markers, as it were—must suffice.

First, Scott's version of the *ordo salutis* reflected a great turn in the federal tradition negotiated by Johannes Cocceius, Dutch Reformed scholar of the mid-seventeenth century, and several generations of followers. Cocceius had sought to develop a fully and strictly biblical account of salvation history in terms of covenant(s). An originally eternal covenant of salvation (*pactum salutis*), he said, had been struck by God the Father and God the Son. This invisible agreement was visibly implemented by a series of divine acts in history, as recounted in scriptural references to successive covenants made with, e.g., Adam, Noah, Abraham, Moses, David, and Jesus Christ. All of these covenants were one and the same with regard to their ultimate origin, substance, and intent; yet each was

[13]The Westminster Confession of Faith, in *Creeds of Christendom*, chap. 7 (ed. Phillip Schaff, 4th ed., rev. and enlarged (Grand Rapids, Mich.: Baker Book House, 1966), 3: pp. 616–617.

distinctive with respect to its specific form and detail, tailored to a specific era (dispensation) of human history. Cocceius apparently conceived of the intratrinitarian pact as an alternative to stress God's eternal decrees of election and reprobation common among self-styled strict Calvinists. This was certainly the role it played in Scott's thought, who did not appeal at this point to Cocceius as an authority.[14] Moreover, Cocceian-like dispensations (Patriarchal, Jewish, and Christian) structure his view of history and scripture as a single but serial-like unfolding drama.[15]

Second, Scott wanted a conditional covenant that upheld the sovereignty, justice, and mercy of God, without the liabilities accrued in the course of disputes over predestinarian doctrines. He was not alone in this wish: the historical Arminius (if not all his "arminian" descendants), the Saumur theologians, Cocceius and his school, and certainly multitudes of Enlightenment era English, Scots, and Americans, wanted much the same. A clean break with predestinarianism was bold action, tantamount to renouncing the Reformed faith. Thus many preferred to evade or modify rather than deny the doctrine. Scott went ahead and made the break, and then spent the rest of his life trying to explain himself, usually by heated invective against Calvinism, but occasionally by working through the issues.

One such attempt came early on in his career, in a four-part series of articles on election in Alexander Campbell's *Christian Baptist* of 1829. Scholastic election, he averred, is "just the old fatalism of the Greeks and Romans" and even more opposed to the progress of the ancient gospel than gross immorality.[16] He then proceeded—one is tempted to say in scholastic fashion—to divide the topic into multiple heads: the elector or electors; the persons elected; the principle on which election is effected; the end or goal to be accomplished by it; when election begins; and when it concludes. His putatively strict biblical answers to these questions required, among other things, reflecting on scripture's varied expressions,

---

[14]Scott describes the *pactum salutis* in a dramatic or hypothetical fashion without using the Latin term or citing any sources, "Election and the 9th Chapter of Romans," *The Evangelist* (1 April 1833): pp. 85–86.

[15]See, e.g., Walter Scott, "Study of the Scriptures, No. 1" *The Evangelist* (1 January 1839): pp. 18–20; and idem, "The Covenants: A Discourse, "*The Evangelist* (1 August 1839): pp. 169–184. The tripartite theme itself appears often in Scott's works, as in those of Alexander Campbell.

[16]Walter Scott, "Election, No. 1," *Christian Baptist* (2 March 1829): pp. 177–179; the remainder of the four-part series appeared in (5 May 1829): pp. 240–243; and (5 October 1829): 69–73 and 73–77. (Pagination follows the revisions of the 2nd ed. of 1835 edited by Davis Staats Burnet, 7 vols. in 1 [Ohio: H. S. Bosworth, 1861]).

five of which—justification from sin, righteousness of God, righteousness of faith, forgiveness of sins, and remission of sins—Scott concluded were virtual synonyms for the same material point. The outcome was not a repudiation of the doctrine of election, but an allegedly revised and improved account of it.

Scott could hardly do without some such alternative account of election. Although human traditions may have garbled the topic, it was neither unbiblical nor superfluous. And easy dismissals of Calvinism brought tactical but hollow victories at best. Even after biblical and rational argument had demolished predestinarianism, the Calvinists still had a trump card left to play: the overthrow of the *decretum horrible* casts the self-styled victor back to works righteousness. This play had always aggravated anti-Calvinists, no end. It drove evangelical Arminians like Wesley, for example, to rhapsodize about prevenient grace.

Reformed theologians were by no means altogether unaware of various problematic features of the conditional covenant they loved so well. Taken at face value, a conditional covenant is in effect a marketplace deal: God will love and bless humans if, and so long as, humans love and obey God. This deal, dress it up as one will, is no way to save sinners. Luther as well as Calvin had detected just that. A promise with strings attached is actually law rather than gospel. It leaves sinners to win or lose God's favor by their own willingness to accept the covenantal conditions and then abide by them. What, then, makes the gospel God's good news to sinners? If it were easy for sinners to accept and keep God's covenantal conditions, divine mercy would be an irrelevancy.

In order then to speak of gospel, one must then take divine law and human sin with utmost seriousness. Over and above covenantal conditions themselves, sinners are in need, something else, namely, the grace of God, to enable them to meet the conditions or forgive them if they do not. Merely easing the conditions and calling the reduced standards "gospel" will not do; this tactic risks depicting God's righteousness as a sliding scale, trivializing the power of sin, and turning God's mercy into a reward for boastful achievement. If there is gospel, it has to involve an empowerment, a force that moves and enables sinful humans to respond in faith. Hence in the Westminster Confession, to the conditional covenant requiring faith in Christ for salvation is added a divine promise of the Holy Spirit "to all those ordained unto life...to make them willing and able to believe."[17]

---

[17]Westminster Confession, chap. 7.

This trump card—the Catch-22 of defeating predestination at the cost of denying the power of grace—is most effectively played, not while theologians like Scott are in the midst of attacking predestinarianism, which is easy to do in modern and postmodern times, but when they propose their own, alternative versions of Christianity's *ordo salutis*. At this point the burden of proof shifts: show how to formulate the conditional covenant in such a way that sinners are not left to save themselves by their own choosing and acting, i.e., their works.

At first glance, Scott's *ordo salutis* fails to meet this challenge, and untold numbers of the Stone-Campbell-Scott movement seem to have liked that first impression best. Faith, repentance, and baptism (by immersion) are the three duties required of humans, and God dutifully responds by granting remission of sins, the gift of the Holy Spirit, and eternal life. So stated, his *ordo* does come across as a formula for works righteousness, legalistic, and (when baptism means immersion of self-declared believers alone) narrow and sectarian as well.

This first glance reading is, I daresay, by no means a total misreading. Scott often hedged his bets, but he made no secret of his opposition to predestinarianism. And when he sought to justify his view, he quickly rounded up the usual suspects—predestination was determinist, speculative, unfair, contrary to divine benevolence and human responsibility, and so on and so forth. The doctrine of limited atonement, a neuralgic point among Reformed theologians themselves, seemed to him especially objectionable. At one point Scott reprinted pages from John Wesley, whom he praised for overthrowing Calvinism.[18] At another point, he attacked the Armenian [*sic*] system too, along with every other human contrivance.[19] No wonder Scott went to such lengths to argue he cared nothing at all about sectarian "isms" and theories—that he cared only about believing and obeying the Bible. He preached in effect "convert today, without delay" and found many willing to do so. And so, at a third point, he advised that the entire dispute was bootless. It sufficed that the *ordo salutis* prove itself in the power of salvation by its effects: try it and experience the benefits that follow.

Perhaps only historical theologians would be inclined to credit Scott for refusing to leave the matter at that. As Scott presented it,

[18]Walter Scott, "Calvinism, No. 2," *The Christian* (1 April 1837): pp. 84–89. See also idem, *The Death of Christ* (improved ed., *The Union of Christians: the Death of Christ*, 2 vols. in 1 [Philadelphia: James Challen and Son, 1864]): 2, pp. 25–28, 38–40.

[19]Scott, *Death of Christ*, pp. 36–37.

the order of salvation is the counterpart, a mirror image, of the order of sin. He developed a schematic analysis of the sixfold plight of sinful humanity: the love of sin, practice of sin, state of sin, guilt of sin, power of sin, and punishment of sin. Each of the six "steps" of his *ordo* corresponded to a portion of sin's multidimensionality.[20] Love of sin is paired with and overcome by faith in Jesus Christ; the practice of sin by repentance, metanoia; the state of sin (alienation from God) by baptism, which is the sign and seal of forgiveness and adoption removing the guilt of sin; the power of sin, by the gift of the Holy Spirit, and the ultimate punishment of sin (eternal death) by resurrection to eternal life.

Given this multidimensional account of human sinfulness, Scott's unwillingness to endorse the high Calvinist codeword "total depravity" seems beside the point: depravity alone sufficed. His references to sin—"a dreadful, abominable evil, horrible thing, a fibrous root, a thready cancer, and a distemper" among them—are by no means indicative of a rosy, favorable, optimistic appraisal of the human condition apart from the promise, means, and power of Godgiven grace.[21] He did affirm, it is true, that fallen humanity retained an instinct for religion, but he insisted that the instinct avails nothing regarding the material content and power of the gospel.[22] He also maintained that fallen humans retain a measure of freedom and that God always deals with them persuasively as rational, moral beings, not coercively.[23] He knew and even cited the Westminster Confession (in order to criticize it) but passed over the passages in it stating much the same.[24] From Scott's account of human sinfulness, then, one gets the impression that his avowedly total and wholehearted break with his Reformed roots was actually only halfhearted, and only half ill-informed.

In his defense, one might note that his reading of "the Calvinistic system" was quite conventional for the day, common to Calvinists and anti-Calvinists alike. Many Reformed theologians, the most skilled and sensitive of them above all, struggled for words to make plain that divine causality was compatible with secondary causality, that neither providence nor predestination was fatalism, that the actuality of sins emerged against the backdrop of the originality of human sinfulness, that empowerment by grace

---

[20]The schematic analysis of sin appears in "Messiah, " *The Evangelist* (2 January 1832): pp. 6–8, and then *Gospel Restored*, p. vi and chap. 18.

[21]See, e.g., Scott, *Gospel Restored*, pp. 90–91, and *Messiahship*, pp. 40–41.

[22]Scott, *Messiahship*, pp. 9–10, 12.

[23]Scott, "Election, No. 4," *Christian Baptist* (5 October 1829): p. 596.

[24]Westminster Confession, chaps. 5, 9–10.

was not ipso facto coercion. It is clear from the length and complexity of his own writings that Scott was preoccupied with the same set of issues as these theologians were, and his complaints about popular Calvinism as well as the "experimental religion of the day (though not all of his proposed remedies) were akin to those voiced by Nevin and Schaff at Mercersburg and Bushnell at Hartford, Connecticut."[25]

At any rate, Scott's "(re)discovery" of the biblical *ordo salutis* was due as much to discontent with church practice as church doctrine. Typical Protestant practice, with or without explicit predestinarianism, had become revivalist. Its aim was to await or—better, if at all possible—to prompt outpourings of the Spirit leading to the rise of faith in the soul. To this end, the unconverted were told to strive mightily to "get religion," and preachers were to strive mightily to assure that all was in place and the stage set for the Spirit to do its work. These mighty human strivings of course looked very much like works righteousness to many true-blue Calvinists. Even so, the successes of revivalism were hard to ignore.

Scott was one of those more impressed by its failings, critical of it for reducing faith to feelings, for leaving those who missed a convulsive born-again experience in despair, and for fostering momentary enthusiasms and commitments that soon faded. The problem, he was convinced, was that everyone had misunderstood the *ordo salutis*. No one has to await or induce *fresh* outpourings of the Spirit. The gospel neither requires nor promises any such immediate, unpredictable operations of the Spirit which, coming supernaturally from beyond, work faith within some sinners and pass over others. His denial of what was then commonly called converting or effectual grace was stunning. In the view of many, friends and foes alike, he had done away with not only creedalism but with the Holy Spirit as well.

Scott himself tried to explain his position, early and often. Certainly, he said, there is the gift of the Holy Spirit. It is what Paul called the Spirit of Christ within—an imparted grace that follows the forensic grace of justification. But imparted grace was bestowed upon baptized, covenant-owning believers alone, not sinners. Its gifts and graces were variously distributed among all those

[25]See, e.g., Walter Scott, "Experimental Religion, No. 1," *Christian Baptist* (5 February 1827): p. 309, and "On Experimental Religion, No. 2," (4 June 1827): p. 309, and "On Experimental Religion, No. 2, " (4 June 1827): pp. 340–341. Parallels such as these are noted in an illumining article by W. Clark Gilpin: "The Doctrine and Thought of Alexander Campbell and John W. Nevin," *Mid-Stream* (October 1980): pp. 417–427.

incorporated into Christ by baptism, enabling them to fulfill their callings as Christians. The work of the Spirit in conversion is another matter.[26]

And make no mistake: for Scott, whose view of nature was totally Newtonian, that is, mechanistic, every operation of the Holy Spirit is *super*natural. Plus, having read the Bible, Scott was well aware that the Spirit blows where it will, and is capable of surprising action. But the *ordo salutis* of the gospel simply does not deal at all with *these* movements of the Spirit. It is an *ordo* ordained by God for the ordinary operations of the Spirit for the ordinary conversion of all too ordinary human sinners. Waiting for, or attempting to induce, fresh outpourings of the Spirit to convert sinners overlooks the fact that the Spirit has already been poured out for them—first in human history and then in the scriptural witness to that history. To expect or demand anything more is not to honor the work of the Spirit but to deny or ignore it.

The bottom-line issue remained: since faith, repentance, and baptism are human acts, the entire formula sounds as though it is crass works righteousness. Under pressure, Scott was often inclined to wave his hand or cite a Bible verse. But he was not altogether without a thoughtful rejoinder. The logic of his *ordo*, I gather, might be put this way.

Faith means faith in Jesus Christ. This faith means acknowledging that salvation is not gained by human effort but by someone other than ourselves, a person with a status and power other and beyond our own. This person is Jesus of Nazareth, who is God's Messiah and Son, the Word of God incarnate, sent by God for the salvation of sinners. Sinful human beings are capable of making such an acknowledgment only because God *enables* them to do so. God performed acts of salvation in history and by the Spirit's inspiration of scripture provided written testimony to those acts. Faith, then, is awakened by hearing and heeding this testimony to God's acts of salvation, which offers its own self-authenticating authority.[27] Those insisting that the Spirit is required to work faith—

[26]See, e.g., Walter Scott, *A Discourse on the Holy Spirit* (2d ed., enlarged and improved, Bethany, Va : Alexander Campbell, 1831), and idem, *Gospel Restored*, sect. 7. His view of the work of the Spirit among baptized believers differs in content from the Westminster Confession not at all.

[27]See, e.g., Scott, *Messiahship*, p. 41: Jesus Christ is "the first and real cause of our regeneration," and "the immediate instumentality is moral, and neither spiritual nor physical...It is the Gospel, which scripture calls the word." Scott's view of multiple causality is nowhere detailed, but rests on an identity-in-difference of God's grace in Christ and mediation of that grace: "Christ's person, then, is the remote cause, and Christ preached the immediate cause, or the instrumentality, in regeneration" (ibid., p. 42).

for "no one can say 'Jesus is Lord' except by the Holy Spirit" (1 Cor. 12:3)—should remember that the Spirit works faith, not directly, immediately, extraordinarily, out-of-the-blue, but in accord with a method of God's design and by way of finite mediation.

Scott had to admit that this work of the Spirit, mediated through the written and preached word is not irresistible, for testimonial evidence is never irresistible. It is nonetheless, he contended, powerful, so powerful on occasion that it sweeps aside objections and not merely elicits but commands assent. So be it, then, with respect to the power of the love of God in Jesus Christ, and indeed Christ crucified for the sake of the world's salvation. Its forcefulness comes by way of the "evidences" given in the Bible.[28] The thrust of Scott's argument is, if the Spirit does not generate faith by means such as this, what would lead anyone to think that it could, or should, do so by any other?

This line of argument looks more simple, perhaps more simplistic, than it actually is. Although it may be taken either as sheer biblicism or sheer rationalism, it also represents a subtle interlacing of several threads of philosophical and theological discussion. One is that of post-Lockean epistemology which based knowledge on the evidentiary force of sense-data and faith on the evidentiary force of eyewitness testimony. The force of sensory evidence is physical, and hence to one degree or another coercive. People do—and so can—deny sensory "realities," but at least some such realities (e.g., human mortality) overwhelm them in the end. That of the latter is intellectual, or moral, and can be resisted more often, easily, and longer. Yet, as the phrase "beyond a reasonable doubt" indicates, testimonial evidence too is, to one degree or another, compelling in a nonphysical way all its own. The other thread is "Word and Spirit," Protestantism's distinctly theological formula for the concurrence of two forces (and norms) which unfortunately seemed to clash as often as they concurred.

To many of its orthodox opponents, Scott's *ordo* of the ancient gospel was at best simply a reassertion of the "Word alone theory," long since tried and found untrue. Yet in insisting on the mediation of grace through the Word as written and preached (and through baptism as well), Scott had tapped into a stream of the Reformed tradition at least as august and arguably older and more genuinely Reformed than the "Calvinist scholasticisms" and the "evangelical revivalisms" he rejected. He himself disavowed all

[28]Scott, *Messiahship*, pp. 14–15.

knowledge of this stream. His own church training as well as (the moderate) Enlightenment thought had schooled him to believe first that "theological orthodoxy" meant immediate rather than mediated grace, and second, that any and every claim of "theological orthodoxy" was to be tested by scripture, as *norma normans sed non normata*.

Christian faith, then, was in Scott's view at one and the same time a rational assent (*fides*) to a simple proposition on the basis of evidentiary testimony of compelling, but not sensorially direct and hence coercive, power and a trusting (*fiducia*) in the object to which that proposition refers. In this case, trust in the referential object of the proposition means trust in a subject, a person—Jesus Christ. Already in Scott's time the most avant-garde thinkers were moving away from—beyond, as they would say—a "propositional" model of revelation. He did not join them, attempting instead (more likely by default than by truly deliberative resolve) to work with, through, and despite a Lockean-Common Sense mentality. Not until the late nineteenth century, long after his death, were attempts such as his considered so outdated as to be naive, ignorant, or disreputable by those well informed about philosophy, theology, natural science, social science, and history. A postcritical view of Scott, it seems to me, could and should "let Scott be Scott." If so, it will not do to reduce his understanding of faith to "Bible-believing" or "rationalism," and then evaluate it according to taste. He aimed by means of his biblical and post-Lockean "confessional propositionalism" at grasping and articulating the *fides quae* and *fides qua* of the Christian church.

The faith Scott proclaimed was rational assent to a single proposition, but not that alone. It was at the same time heartfelt trust in salvation through the person and work of Jesus, "Christ," "Son of God," and Savior. Scott's *ordo salutis* made confessing this faith a presupposition for, and condition of, salvation. But this confession presupposed, and was conditional upon, the "reality" of salvation by the grace of God incarnate in Jesus Christ and the evidentiary force of the writings ("scriptures") of witnesses inspired by God the Spirit to testify to this reality.

Once someone acknowledges something as a reality, things change. The human situation changes. Awareness of the reality of the love of God in Christ brings just such a change. In the Bible it is called repentance (*metanoia*), which is a turning, a change of life orientation. Humans, sinners all, are capable of this change only in the sense that once love for God is awakened in them, they cannot do other than break off their affairs with other loves, regretting that they had for so long wooed and served other objects of desire and resolve to commit themselves to a change of life. And this resolve leads them to action.

In Scott's *ordo salutis*, the key action is baptism, a sign marking a change of state or condition. By this Scott means not a change with regard to human nature, but a change of relationship and, as it were, status between the sinful human and the merciful God who saves sinners. To be baptized is, of course, an act of obedience. Humans are capable of this action, however, only because a dominant principle of conviction, once lodged in the heart, becomes a trigger to action. Loving Christ because he first loved us, believers attest to their love by their actions. Yet baptism is also God's act: it is the means by which God provides assurance of remission of sins, justification, and incorporation and adoption in Christ. Then comes point five. By the gift of the Holy Spirit, grace imputed in baptism becomes grace imparted in the lives of believers, and point six, hope in God's promise of resurrection and eternal life.

This pattern of correlations reflects an anthropology which, however ancient or even biblically based, held sway in the British Enlightenment and Scottish Common Sense thought, in particular. A human being is constituted in such a way that the dominant principles of the mind govern the inclinations of the heart, which in turn orient the self to one goal or another and therefore lead to an appropriate course of action.

What Scottish Common Sense philosophy—or any other "human wisdom" for that matter, in Scott's view—failed to supply was both the material content of Christian faith as told in the "story" of salvation—history and the power of God that made that story true to life in the cases of countless sinners. Scott's own remorseless emphasis on messiahship drove him to reflect often on the death of Jesus. His thoughts on the subject were directed, from first to last, by the Pauline theme of Christ crucified. He compressed the material into a thesis statement: God lays the sin of Adam on all, and the sins of all on Christ.[29] And this plunged him into one of the most controverted issues of the history of theology, the doctrine of atonement.

The death of Jesus was, of course, an event in history like any other. To understand just this much about it, however, is to miss the point of the gospel altogether. As it relates to good news from

---

[29]Scott, *Death of Christ*, pp. 21, 74.

God, it is—Scott himself put it—"pregnant of purpose."[30] The Bible speaks of its multiple meanings, now in narrative, now in poetic, now in didactic forms of presentation. Scott's aim, then, like that of almost every other Christian theologian, was to grasp the meaning of the many meanings, and his thesis—God lays the sin of Adam on all and the sin of all on Christ—was intended to do just that.[31] This formulation of the problem with, and remedy for, the human condition reveals Scott the legendary frontier evangelist to be Scott the Pauline traditionalist theologian as well, even though precisely because his thesis was "biblical" he denied it was traditional or theological.

The result nonetheless was a federal theology of the cross. God relates to humanity by means of covenanting, and the individuals who enter into covenant do so not merely as individuals but as representative leaders of many. Thus the story of Adam is not Adam's story alone, the first human, but the story of the state of humanity as such: for all who are human are *coram deo* like him, with him, and in him. Augustine, centuries after Paul and many more centuries before Scott, accounted for the generalizable representativeness of Adam in terms of the biological, quasi-hereditary transmission of sin, guilt, and death upon the descendants of Adam and Eve. The federal tradition of theology, many centuries after Augustine and a few before Scott, shifted its account of the story's meaning from premodern biology to early modern politics: just as the fortunes of an entire people rise or fall along with the rise or fall of the sovereign, the head of leadership who represents them and their interests, so too the fortunes of all humanity turned on the fall of Adam, their representative, covenantal leader.

The fall of Adam is, then, representative of the fallenness of all humanity. Out of mercy, however, God has granted humanity another representative, a new federal head, a new Adam, through whom comes forgiveness of sins, the gift of the Holy Spirit, and hope of life eternal. The work of Christ is manifold, each of its aspects correlated to one or another aspect of the sin of Adam. The most detailed of Scott's correlations of the two forms a long list.[32]

Scott's lists, though *ad seriatim*, saved him from fixing on any single text, image, or theory of atonement. Yet he was no more

[30]Ibid., p. 12.

[31]Ibid. , pp. 10–12, 21.

[32]Scott, *Messiahship*, pp. 34–38, on the regal, paternal, and generic headship of Christ; see also his statements in *Death of Christ*, pp.10–12, 16–18, 22–25.

content with an undifferentiated assortment of meanings than any other theologian. Two themes emerged as most critical in his thought. One was the theme of blood sacrifice for the propitiation of sins. This line of thinking, prominent in old Protestant orthodoxy, has come to be known as the penal substitutionary theory of the atonement. Equally prominent in Scott's account of the atonement is another theme—a governmental theory. It was an old, post-Reformation theme gaining exceptional currency among Calvinists and anti-Calvinists alike in the late eighteenth and early nineteenth centuries. Scott collated the two themes (as well as others) by privileging the latter: propitiation means "to do honor to the majesty of law and the character of God as ruler."[33]

Its starting point is an image of God as a ruler of the world, wise, benevolent, just, and merciful, who establishes and upholds laws for the well-being of every subject. Human sin is, along with all else it is, a violation of the principle of divine government itself. As such it demands justice, redress, in this case eternal death. The mercy of God is shown by God defering this punishment and providing the redress. Jesus Christ, the Son of God incarnate, takes on sin and bears its death penalty as humanity's federal representative. His death, then, is a work of mercy effecting forgiveness of sins for the sake of many. Indeed, it is the work of manifold mercy that effects reconciliation with God, honors and fulfills the demands of divine justice, and reinforces on the hearts and minds of sinners the justness of justice. Simply put, Scott preached and taught justification for sinners by grace through faith in Jesus Christ, and the gift of the Spirit, new life, and hope of life eternal as well. But this grace of God has come at the cost of the passion of Christ which is, at the same time, the self-giving of God.

However one might judge Scott's federalism, the judgment should recognize that his was one antebellum federalism among many others, far more traditionalist and indeed Reformed if not more residually Calvinist than he himself recognized. In any case, the one thing that cannot rightly be said of his thought is that it was not theology.

---

[33]This statement climaxes the exposition in *The Gospel Restored*, pp. 79–86; further comment is made there, pp. 188–191, 197–211, 483–515. See also idem, "On the Death of Christ," *The Evangelist* (October 1834): 217–219; (December 1834): 275–278; (March 1835): 49–52; (April 1835): 103–106; and (June 1835): 131–132; as well as idem, "Death of Christ," pp. 47–48, 55–56, 59–61, 64–71. John Mark Hicks has provided valuable studies of Scott and his theological context: "Atonement Theology in the Late Nineteenth Century: The Pattern of Discussion within the Stone-Campbell Movement," *Discipliana* (Winter 1966): 116–127; and "What Did Christ Accomplish on the Cross? Atonement in Campbell, Stone, and Scott," *Lexington Theological Quarterly* (Fall 1995): 145–170.

CHAPTER FOUR

Walter Scott as Biblical Interpreter

Thomas H. Olbricht

Walter Scott's early years in Scotland were crucial no doubt in providing the foundations for his later interpretation of the biblical text. His parents, John and Mary Innes Scott, were members of the Church of Scotland; in other words, they were Presbyterians. Whatever specific preaching Walter heard was likely focused on the biblical text. Thomas F. Torrance in his book on Scottish theology attributed a new emphasis on biblical exposition to Robert Rollock (1555–99) of Edinburgh,

> There was another side, however, to Robert Rollock as "Minister of the Evangel of Jesus Christ" as he preferred to be called, even when principal of the College of Edinburgh. This was his concern for biblical exposition which he introduced into Scottish universities, and, not least his regular preaching of the gospel in line with the tradition of John Knox and Robert Bruce. The importance he gave to biblical exposition was very evident in his commentaries on the epistles of St. Paul to the Romans,

> Galatians, Ephesians, Colossians, Thessalonians, Philemon, and the Epistle to the Hebrews...[1]

These commentaries, standard fare for the time, were essentially published as preached and in fact were frequently recorded by a stenographer, corrected by the preacher, and then printed.

Another characteristic of the preaching, varying with the preacher, was a structured, rationalistic approach. This approach may be attributed to Peter Ramus (1515–1572) at an earlier stage, but it also took later forms. Torrance observed in conjunction with Rollock's affirmation that the covenant was two way and did not depend on grace but the observance of the stipulations, that,

> The general effect of all this was that faith was intellectualised, theology was logicalised, and the Christian life was moralised. These tendencies, the federal scheme of salvation, the moralising of the Christian life, and the intellectualising of faith, the logicalising of theology, passed into Scottish theology...[2]

As an example, Torrance set out the structure of a work by David Dickson (1583–1663) and James Durham (1622–58) *The Sum of Saving Knowledge.*

> *The Sum of Saving Knowledge* may be taken up in these four heads: 1. The woeful condition wherein all men are by nature, through breaching the covenant of works. 2. The remedy provided for the elect in Jesus Christ by the covenant of grace. 3. The means appointed to make them partakers of this covenant. 4. The blessings which are effectually conveyed unto the elect by these means—Which four heads are set down each of them in some few propositions.[3]

Walter Scott later exhibited these same propensities in his own schematization of biblical history and salvation.

Another characteristic of Scottish theology worthy of note is its focus upon the unity of God's purposes flowing out of the Old

---

[1]Thomas F. Torrance, *Scottish Theology from John Knox to John McLeod Campbell* (Edinburgh: T&T Clark, 1996), p. 62.

[2]Ibid.

[3]Ibid., p. 112.

Testament into the New. Likewise, the focus upon the church, and Christ as its founder, should be noted and remembered.

> Throughout the theology of the Scottish Reformation, there is the strongest sense of the continuity of the Christian Church with Israel, the Old Testament people of God, for it is the same mighty living God who acts in both. But there is a difference marked by the Incarnation.
>
> First, the Old Testament Church was tied to the temple, its cult, and its institutions, although the destruction of the tabernacle and then of the temple was an indication from God that the Church has its real existence beyond. But that was not evident until New Testament times. The New Testament Church has its being and ground in Jesus Christ.[4]

As Torrance wrote of John Knox, "...the Church...has a succession which stretches from creation to the Second Advent of Christ in unbroken continuous being."[5] Furthermore, the Bible itself sets out in a broad sweep the fate of the church from the time of Christ until his coming again. Scott claims to come upon these emphases on his own, in his effort to discern what God had done, and is doing, in this world. But it is likely not accidental that what he discovered was not far distant from what he heard in the churches of his upbringing.

Scott at Edinburgh

In 1812 Walter Scott's parents arranged for him to enroll at the University of Edinburgh, in hopes that he would enter the ministry of the Church of Scotland. At sixteen, he was perhaps a year or two older than the conventional age for matriculation. Dwight E. Stevenson learned from the librarian at the University of Edinburgh that the curriculum for the first year consisted of Latin, Greek, logic, metaphysics, mathematics, and moral philosophy.[6] Scott probably also took Hebrew, divinity, ecclesiastical history, natural philosophy, universal civil history and antiquities, rhetoric, and belles lettres before he was through.[7] The bachelor of arts program

---

[4]Ibid., p. 28.

[5]Ibid., p. 27.

[6]Dwight E. Stevenson, *Walter Scott: Voice of the Golden Oracle: A Biography* (St. Louis: Christian Board of Publication, 1946).

[7]William A. Gerrard III, *A Biographical Study of Walter Scott: American Frontier Evangelist* (Joplin: College Press, 1992), p. 19.

contained no courses in biblical studies as is now taught. Scripture may have been the basis for learning Greek or Hebrew but was translated with little exegetical comment.

Scott apparently stayed for six years, until 1818. The requirement was six years in succession, and in Edinburgh four months of the year. As the students grew older they likely spent part of the year teaching.[8] At that time there were three professorships of theology: Divinity, Hebrew and Oriental Languages, and Ecclesiastical History.[9] It was not until after the commission of 1826–30 that the Bachelor of Divinity was upgraded at Edinburgh. The chair of Biblical Criticism and Antiquities, though proposed earlier, was not occupied until 1847.[10] By 1876 the B.D. could be taken in all four Scottish universities, with candidates from religious backgrounds other than the Church of Scotland.

Scott replicated the same approach to Greek translation with his three pupils in the school of George Forrester. He wrote, referring to himself in the third person, "...in 1820 he appointed three of his pupils to commit, repeat, and translate the gospels in the Greek language."[11] Scott's knowledge of exegetical studies was therefore probably acquired when he inherited the library of George Forrester upon the latter's death in 1820. Scott reported that the Forrester library included Benson on the epistles, [James] McKnight's *Harmony of the Gospels*, Catchbull's *Notes*, [George] Campbell on the four Gospels, McKnight on the epistles, and Bishop Newcomb's *Harmony of the Gospels*. Scott's foray into biblical studies was therefore essentially like that of all his Scottish, and in fact, American contemporaries, until the studies of a decade later when seminary education blossomed.

How are we to evaluate the biblical scholars upon which Scott drew? Alexander Campbell purchased and read the major biblical scholars of the time, for example, J. A. Ernesti (1707–1781),

---

[8]*Dictionary of Scottish Church History & Theology*, ed. Nigel M. de S. Cameron (Downers Grove: InterVarsity Press, 1993), p. 281.

[9]It is interesting in this regard to note that at Bacon College in Georgetown, Kentucky, of which Scott was identified as the first President, in the faculty listing he was identified as "President and Professor of Hebrew Literature." No professor of New Testament was listed, but the same faculty positions in respect to scripture would have also been the case at Harvard and other American colleges, as also was apparently true in Scotland.

[10]*Disruption to Diversity, Edinburgh Divinity 1846–1996*, ed. David F. Wright and Gary D. Badcock (Edinburgh: T&T Clark, 1996), pp. 54, 55.

[11]Walter Scott, *The Messiahship or Great Demonstration, Written for the Union of Christians, on Christian Principles, as Plead for in the Current Reformation* (Cincinnati: H. S. Bosworth, 1859), p. 6.

J. D. Michaelis (1717–1791) and F. A. G. Tholuck (1799–1877) in Germany, Thomas Hartwell Horne (1780–1862) in Great Britain, and Moses Stuart (1780–1852) in America. Scott, in contrast, mostly read those with whom he first became acquainted. As far as we can ascertain, some of the major exegetical scholars to whom he was drawn through the years were:

Norton Catchbull (1601–1684), Cambridge
John Locke (1632–1704), Oxford, London
Isaac Newton (1642–1727), Cambridge
William Warburton (1698–1779), Gloucester
George Benson (1699–1764), Glasgow
George Campbell (1719–1796), Aberdeen
James MacKnight (1721–1800), Edinburgh
William Newcomb (1729–1800), Armagh
John Towers (1747–1894), London
Thomas Hartwell Horne (1780–1862), London

Two-thirds of these scholars died before Scott was born. These men were admired in Scotland and Great Britain, but by the 1830s, at which time Scott launched a flurry of publications, they were already superseded by the Germans, except that the sum of their translations of biblical texts into English remained the best available. They mostly published translations, harmonies of the gospels, paraphrases, notes, and annotations.

However, Scott was well read in contemporary authors, whatever his inadequacies may have been in biblical studies. He read with approbation: "Selden, Chillenworth, Boileau, Hale, Boyle, Milton, Cowper, Brown, Bacon, Romaine, Littleton, Paley, Locke, Cudworth, Clarke, Doddridge, Lardner, Robertson, Butler, Watts, Campbell, McKnight, Addison, Beattie, Boerhaave, Burnet, Collins, Erskine, Euler, Fenelon, Tillotston, Grotius, Sir Humphrey Davy, and others."[12] He also mentioned as unbelievers: Bollinbroke, Hume, Voltaire, Gibbon, Rousseau, Chesterfield, Godwin, Hobbes, D'Alembert, Diderot, Thomas Paine, along with other celebrated leaders of the crowd of infidels.[13]

---

[12]Walter Scott, *The Gospel Restored. A Discourse of the True Gospel of Jesus Christ, in which the Facts, Principles, Duties, and Privileges of Christianity are Arranged, Defined, and Discussed, and the Gospel in its various Parts Shown to be Adapted to the Nature and Necessities of Man in his Present Condition* (Cincinnati: Ormsby H. Donogh, 1836), p. 237.

[13]Ibid., pp. 318, 319.

The Biblical Focus of Scott

It is not fully clear what led Walter Scott away from the hopes of his parents that he become a minister in the Church of Scotland. It seems when he came to America he was more interested in teaching than in being a minister. His own personal focus on life before God resulted from his friendship with George Forrester who ran a school and was minister of a congregation of Scottish Baptists in Pittsburgh, Pennsylvania. In 1819, Forrester immersed Scott, who then became a member of the small congregation. So while Scott refocused his faith, it was all within the context of his Scottish Presbyterian upbringing. Forrester seems specifically to have been influenced by the Scottish evangelists Robert Haldane 1764–1842 and James Haldane 1768–1851.

It would be surprising if Scott had not heard of James Haldane, who in 1801 commenced preaching in Edinburgh at the "Tabernacle" and continued at the same location until his death. It is also probable that Forrester read the works of John Glas (1695–1773) and Robert Sandeman (1718–1771) since Scott mentioned them specifically as being in Forrester's library.[14] All four of these independent Scottish church leaders were well known within the context in which Scott grew up. John MacLeod, in his book on Scottish theology, shows that an intellectual approach to faith flourished in the Edinburgh of Scott's day, advocated by John Erskine (1721–1803) as well as Thomas Chalmers (1780–1847). They wished, much like Scott, to include emotions, though secondary to understanding.

> Dr. Erskine laid such a stress on the essentially intellectual side of man's being, but he was emphatic in the point that his view of the matter was not that of the Glassites. He held that faith is radically belief of the truth, and this is an exercise of the understanding by way of assent. He went on, however, to teach that what is rooted in our exercise of the understanding goes on to function as an exercise of the emotional powers and of the will so that as the result of the initial assent there springs up a consent of the heart.[15]

---

[14]Walter Scott, *The Messiahship*, p. 7.

[15]John MacLeod, *Scottish Theology in Relation to Church History Since the Reformation* (Edinburgh: Banner of Truth Trust, 1974 reprint; 1st ed. 1943), p. 187. He also mentions this as the approach of the "old Scots Baptists."

Study of Walter Scott has mostly placed him in the context of Scottish and British philosophy. Such study is of merit. But in order to understand the larger parameters of Scott's thought I have recently been impressed with the need to read him against the backdrop of Scottish theology. I have now concluded that he was much more indebted to the major Scottish visions than he himself realized. We have perhaps been misled by Scott when he wrote about his discovery of the "Ancient Gospel," for this was only a limited aspect of the larger picture. For example, he stated in the first volume of *The Evangelist*,

> I had been a Presbyterian, but my mind now became wholly revolutionized and sunk down like lead, upon the first principles of the gospel, as may be seen in a few essays which I had the pleasure of writing for the periodical of our distinguished Bro. Alexander Campbell about 10 years ago…I had consulted no mortal on the topic of the ancient gospel, the very phrase was unknown, except in a single piece, which was dropt from *my own pen* about two or three months before. I was prompted to it by no man nor set of men, nor did I get it from men, but from the book of God, and that too by a course of reading, meditation, and prayer to God, which he alone knows, and to him alone the praise is due.[16]

Forrester drowned in 1820 and Scott succeeded him both as teacher and minister. In these years he read those passages of the Bible which especially focused upon Jesus as Messiah and the salvation of humankind. In 1821 he read a pamphlet on baptism by Henry Errett, of New York City. He was so impressed that he traveled to New York to visit the congregation there which Robert Richardson believed was Haldanian, but may also have had Sandemanian influences.[17]

As with all who study the Bible, Scott was interested in some parts more than others. He was especially focused on the corporate side of reality rather than the individual. One might go on to say that, more than any other feature of Christianity, he was interested in what is now designated biblical anthropology. His understanding of salvation was premised upon a prior understanding

---

[16]Walter Scott, *The Evangelist* (2 April 1832): pp. 93, 94.

[17]Robert Richardson, *Memoirs of Alexander Campbell* (1897; reprint, Nashville: The Gospel Advocate Company, 1956), p. 505.

of humankind in regard to sin and the search for happiness. Salvation resulted from the work of Christ for all humankind, and in turn is fully realized in the body of believers, the church. God likewise is working for human improvement in the body politic.

These basic predispositions are Scottish in orientation. They reflect the corporate perspective on soteriology, ecclesiology, and government. Scott's biblical anthropology also shared many of the presuppositions of contemporary Scottish moral philosophy. He was much more interested in fleshing out these realities in the narrative parts of the Bible than in explicating them from legal or epistolary materials. For this reason, Scott spent most of his time, especially in his books, commenting on Genesis, Exodus, and the gospels. Of secondary importance were Acts, the Old Testament histories, Daniel, and the Revelation. Scott drew very little on the epistles, or Leviticus, Numbers, Proverbs, and the Psalms.

When Scott first examined the Bible in depth, according to his own report, he worked on the gospels, except Luke, and with his three students translated them from Greek. At the same time he spent two years studying the gospels with the Pittsburgh church. Again, speaking of himself in the third person, he wrote:

> He will only state that the matter which first turned his attention to the great proposition was very probably the fact that, in 1820, he appointed three of his pupils to commit, repeat, and translate the gospels in the Greek language. They succeeded in committing Matthew, Mark, and John… He also taught twice a week in his little church the same gospels for twenty-two months at a stretch, and in his admiration for the great revelation wrote in large letters with chalk over the door of his academy, that he might teach it to his pupils—"Jesus is the Christ"… It is not claimed by any one that he restored to the church or the world the great oracle that "Jesus is the Christ." But if there is in Christendom any body of people who presents that proposition as the problematical element of the gospel exclusively, if any section of the Christian profession offers it in its practical forms as the basis of Christian union, the symbol of confession for the remission of sins, and the element of our perfection in holiness, save our brethren, the author is not aware of it.[18]

[18]Walter Scott, *The Messiahship*, p. 5.

Scott obviously came to view the messiahship of Christ as the key to Christianity, the Christian church, and salvation, but in his major writings he spent much more time in Genesis than in the gospels.

As to his approach to history, Scott clearly conceived the text of the Bible, the Old Testament as well as the New, as setting forth the authentic report on the actions of God and humanity. He didn't even entertain the prospect, so commonly embraced by biblical scholars today, that the real history must be reconstructed from biblical and extrabiblical sources. Carl Holladay set out this contrast in *The New Interpreter's Bible,*

> Whereas the locus of revelation in the divine oracle paradigm is within the text itself, in the historical paradigm it tends to shift outside the text. Rather than reading the words of scripture, and expecting to hear the word of God coming directly through the sacred page, or through the sacred story unfolded in the sacred page, the reader now looks behind or beyond, the biblical text to another story that is independent of the biblical text.[19]

Scott was interested in sin and salvation as a plot, a drama, the great divine narrative. It was for this reason that he focused on those materials in the Bible which exhibited narrativity. The opening of *The Gospel Restored* demonstrates this predilection.

> The fall of man, and his recovery by Jesus Christ our Lord forms a great drama, of which God is the author. The chief personage is the Messiah, and his mighty and subtle antagonist is an archangel in arms. The parties are demons and angels, the theatre is the universe, the stage the world, and its government the subject in debate. The plot lies in bringing good out of evil, happiness out of misery, almighty power from feminine weakness, light out of darkness, glory from the grave. The catastrophe consists of the seizure and perdition of the traitor angel with all his powers, and of the final triumph of the Son of Man with all his saints.[20]

---

[19]Carl R. Holladay, "Contemporary Methods of Reading the Bible," *The New Interpreter's Bible*, Vol. 1 (Nashville: Abingdon, 1994), p. 128.

[20]Scott, *The Gospel Restored*, p. 9.

It is clear in his introduction to *The Messiahship* that Scott saw this drama as corporate—a drama for all of humankind.

> The book is the fruit of a protracted and devout study of the mission of our Lord Jesus Christ to the Jewish nation. The author having assumed the Messiahship of our Lord Jesus Christ as the center of the Christian system, and placed himself as it were in that center, has for nearly forty years waited on its gradual development in his own mind...[21]

The Use of Scripture

As we have already seen, Scott regarded his studies in the Bible as involving more than ferreting out the conclusions of others. In some sense he viewed his biblical scholarship as uniquely his own. He made this declaration in various places. In his studies of the millennium which engrossed his efforts especially in the late 1830s and 1840s he declared his own independent investigations of grounds previously traversed by others.

> Being, some years ago, dissatisfied with the modern and popular doctrine of a millennium, because it seemed to us to interfere with the proper hope of the gospel, namely: the coming of our Lord Jesus Christ from heaven, and the resurrection of the dead, and because it taught professors to look for a triumphant state of christianity in the present evil world, before the appearance of our Lord Jesus Christ, we entered with great care upon the consideration of this subject. [22]

Was Scott correct in his assessment that he was in some sense a different sort of biblical scholar? If so, it was not so much in method. His approach to the text was much the same as that of his contemporaries. He studied the text in the original languages, as well as translations. He employed the standard lexicographical and grammatical works. His hermeneutical principles were much the same, influenced by the British empirical Enlightenment tendency for generalizations from a series of specifics. But Scott viewed these specifics from the context of the work of God down through history and into the future. He had a clearly worked out scheme of

[21]Scott, *The Messiahship*, p. 5.

[22]Scott, *The Evangelist* (1 October 1841): p. 217.

redemption which covered human prehistory, history, and post-history. Even these schemes were dependent on those already worked out in Scottish theology.

So what was unique about Scott's biblical studies? He was correct that he did not necessarily come out in the same place as either his associates or prior scholars. And when he finished his work, some of his own unique insights and approaches were stamped on the results. The unique traits were the specifics of the schematizations and the ways in which Scott reflected on the text in regard to positions taken by his contemporaries. Scott was both shrewd and creative in setting out his particular slant and in the characteristics of his arguments and refutations.

The approaches of Scott will be set out more specifically by first examining the manner in which he constructed and communicated the ancient gospel. Next we will ascertain the way he employed the biblical text in certain of his polemic writings. Finally we take a look at Scott's schematization of the divine drama, as he mapped the unfolding of history, past, present, and future, or God's scheme of redemption.

The Plan of Salvation

In 1836 Scott believed his chief contribution to the fledgling restoration movement was his clarity in presenting the "Ancient Gospel." This gospel was not defined so much by the life of Jesus, but rather by the gospel plan of salvation, something Scott also designated as "the first principles of the Gospel."[23] He wrote in the introduction to *The Gospel Restored*:

> The present century, then, is characterized by these three successive steps, which the lovers of our Lord Jesus have been enabled to make, in their return to the original institution. First, the Bible was adopted as sole authority in our assemblies, to the exclusion of all other books. Next the Apostolic order was proposed. Finally the True Gospel was restored.[24]

The plan of salvation commenced with the faith that Jesus is the Messiah, the Son of God. This beginning point informs the teaching and preaching of the church not only in regard to the ancient gospel, but also in respect to the ancient order.

---

[23]Scott, *The Evangelist* (2 April 1832): p. 93.
[24]Scott, *The Gospel Restored*, pp. v, vi.

> JESUS—First, the grand fundamental proposition, "Is Jesus the Christ." He who would be master of assemblies must discuss this, times and ways without number: then his natural character as Son of God: then his official character, as prophet, priest, and king; the principles of the Ancient Gospel, beginning with faith; the Ancient Order, beginning with the article of worship, & birth, life, ministry, poverty, zeal, obedience, humiliation, transfiguration, trial, confession, condemnation, death, burial, and resurrection, ascension, glorification in heaven, the prophecies, miracles, with the external and internal evidences of our religion.[25]

Scott wrote much about the gospel plan of salvation, but to get a quick picture of his perspectives one must turn to his schematic presentation.

> *A Classification of Duties and Privileges.*
>
> The kingdom of God—its privileges and blessing are conditional by duty. It is duty first and privilege afterward.
>
> *Duties*
>
> 1. Faith. 2. Repentance. 3. Baptism.
>
> *Privileges*
>
> 1. Remission of Sins. 2. The Holy Spirit. 3. Eternal Life.[26]

In a less schematic form, earlier Scott had written,

> In other words, brethren, to make us see the beauty and perfection of the gospel theory as devised by God; faith is to destroy the love of sin, repentance to destroy the practice of it, baptism the state of it, remission the guilt of it, the Spirit the power of it, and the resurrection to destroy the punishment of sin; so that the last enemy, death, will be destroyed.[27]

In setting out the order, Scott stressed especially the positioning of the receiving of the Holy Spirit. Faith was produced, not by the Spirit as most evangelicals believed, but by testimony establishing Jesus's Messiahship. "The Spirit...was uniformly given to those who believed and obeyed the Gospel, not to produce faith,

---

[25]Scott, *The Evangelist* (2 April 1832): p. 104.

[26]Scott, *The Messiahship*, p. 293.

[27]Scott, *The Gospel Restored*, p. vi.

but to reward it."[28] Or on the same matter he wrote, "The Holy Spirit is also a blessing given and bestowed on the obedient after baptism, but never before faith."[29]

How is the believer quickened by the Spirit? Scott answered:

> Is it by special and distinct operations upon the mind of the sinner before faith, as all your systems of divinity assert? Or does he, for the purpose of producing faith and life in us, adduce testimony—divine testimony of the holy scripture? We Reformers assert the latter as the true state of the case, and it is a proposition which derives proof and illustration from every individual conversion noticed in scripture; a proposition in harmony, as well with fact and scripture, as with reason and the common experience of mankind. Is it in the annals of humanity, that men, endowed with the reasonability common to their species, ever obtained faith in anything earthly or divine, but by means of testimony?[30]

But Scott wanted to make clear that the Spirit actually came to dwell in the believer rather than a believer simply receiving the word of God. The Spirit, for Scott, was not synonymous with the word of God.

> When Bro. John S_____ was preaching, shortly after the public restoration of the immersion of remission, he was asked what he meant by the Holy Spirit, for he urged the people to be baptized that they might receive the Holy Spirit, he answered that he meant the word of God—for he did not believe the Spirit was any thing distinct from the word. Then replied Bro. M______, you should say, and the people would understand you, "Be baptized every one of you in the name of Jesus Christ for the remission of your sins, and you shall receive a New Testament."[31]

Though Scott presented the ancient gospel as a formula, he wanted to make it clear that it was the gospel of the living Christ,

---

[28]Scott, *The Evangelist* (4 March, 1832): p. 56.
[29]Scott, *The Messiahship,* p. 294.
[30]Scott, *The Evangelist* (5 February 1832): p. 27.
[31]Scott, *The Evangelist* (2 September 1833): p. 210.

with consequences touching on morality and faith, and not merely a logical progression.

> It is a fact that many have adopted this theory and in their speaking about it do but little good. It is a lamentable fact indeed that we have some *"bare-bone proclaimers,"* theoretical to a hair-breadth, and proclaimers of water rather than of Christ, that talk of baptism for the remission of sins, until every body is sick of it. These brethren forgetting the double use of the arrangement, forgetting that it is intended by the gracious remission and blessing and hope which it contains, to reconcile the world to God, see nothing in it but an instrument to confute Sectarianism and consequently rave away about other professors until every body is ready to quit the house, but I hope our churches as they attain better order will be more careful and sustain in their labours not those who rave about the scaffolding but those, who on the solid foundation of this arrangement, build that superstructure of morals and faith which is found in the whole New Testament.[32]

At the same time, Scott wanted to make clear that he was not apologetic about having a theory.

> Indeed! We preach *Christ*, not a *theory*; but after all, to argue for a theory and to preach it, are very distinct things: none ought to preach a theory; none can preach without one: we preach not the theory of the Ancient Gospel! but only Christ according to that theory; and it is indispensable that, that and all others abroad should be brought to the test of Scripture, and proved to be that, according to which Paul preached Christ; for you have seen that Paul himself had a theory, and consequently was a theorist.[33]

In these schematic materials Scott gave deference to scripture, but did not make specific references. In the fleshed out versions of the "Ancient Gospel," how did Scott bring passages from the Bible to bear? In the 1836 book *The Gospel Restored*, Scott, to show what he perceived to be the state of humankind, presented a section

---

[32]Scott, *The Evangelist* (6 August 1832): p. 182.
[33]Ibid. (3 September 1832): p. 194.

"Concerning Sin." [34] This was Scott's favorite way of describing the sinner and he no doubt employed it often in his evangelistic preaching. The succession of topics was as follows: 1. Of the desire or love of sin; 2. Of the practice of sin; 3. Of the state of sin; 4. Of the guilt of sin; 5. Of the power of sin; 6. Of the punishment of sin. Scripture is sprinkled throughout this material by way of both quotation and allusion, but interestingly with no chapter and verse identifications.

Scott employed the Bible in two ways, one of which was to offer examples. His examples came from the Bible, not from contemporary life, but in effect, in a Bible civilization, persons in the Bible are contemporaries. Most of his examples were from the Old Testament: Adam, Eve, Lot's wife, Noah, Absalom; with one from the New, the Ethiopian Eunuch. The examples therefore came from Genesis, Exodus, 2 Samuel, and the Acts. Other passages were employed as proof texts, most frequently statements from or about Jesus. These came from Genesis, the Psalms, Matthew, Hebrews, and the Revelation. A typical statement corroborated by a text is, "The less apparently the sin, the greater in reality the danger. At all events 'He that is unfaithful in the least is unfaithful also in that which is greatest.'" In this section Scott did not enter into an extended exposition of a narrative text as he did elsewhere on occasion.

In chapters of *The Gospel Restored* titled, "Faith and Confession," "Faith and Evidence," and "The Kingdom of Heaven," some thirty pages, Scott turned more to the New Testament.[35] His main concern was to show that faith should be demonstrated in life, that it was based on evidence, and that God's premier work on earth is manifested in the kingdom, that is, the church. The import of the Bible is conspicuous throughout these chapters. Scott brings in texts as proof, examples, words to encourage actions, and as allusions, for example, that crooked things cannot be made straight. Of the passages brought to bear, a large majority are in the Gospel of John. Matthew takes second place while the Acts, Romans, 1 and 2 Corinthians, Hebrews, and 1 Peter are cited a few times each. In the Old Testament references are made to Genesis, the Psalms, and Job, as well as a long quote from Ecclesiastes 12. In the rest of the New Testament may be found Mark, Luke, Ephesians, Colossians, Philippians, 1 John, and the Revelation. Again there is no exposition of a lengthy narrative text, an approach Scott uses with some frequency in other arguments.

---

[34]Scott, *The Gospel Restored*, pp. 39–41.

[35]Ibid., pp. 192–224.

Polemical Writings

While much of the writing of Scott is polemical, that found in his journal, *The Evangelist*, is especially so.[36] It is therefore appropriate to assess his employment of scripture in such pieces. In 1841, on a visit to Pittsburgh, Scott was given a book by a church member written by a Presbyterian minister, John T. Pressly, living in Pittsburgh. The book treated the topic of Christian baptism.[37] Scott published a review, or reply, in five parts.[38] The first two parts, which comprise about eighty percent of the review, contain all the major arguments.

Scott's first concern was that Pressly contended infants were a proper subject of baptism. Pressly admitted that Mark 16:16 could not be employed to support infant baptism since "He that believeth and is baptized" cannot apply to infants, and in this conclusion, Scott declared that Pressly had no dispute with the Baptists. Pressly rather established the case for infant baptism by declaring that in former dispensations infants were ceremonially inducted into the people of God. Therefore, they should be so inducted through infant baptism in the Christian dispensation. In the Jewish dispensation the mark of entry was circumcision, and in the Christian, at the same age, baptism. Scott readily agreed with Pressly's three covenants: the Patriarchic, the Jewish, and the Christian. But he contended they need not be identical in requirements.

Pressly charged that the opponents to infant baptism should prove that infants in the Christian dispensation are to be cut off. The inclusion of infants, Scott replied, is not obvious in the Bible. Those who contend for infant baptism must prove infant membership in the church from the New Testament. To this point Scott did not advance any scripture, but his reflection did assume that the Bible contained what was commonly accepted at the time—three dispensations. He proceeded to deduce certain arguments from the threefold eras which biblical scholars of the time commonly agreed were contained in the Bible.

Scott felt it necessary to establish that Israelite infants were circumcised by command in the law of Moses. He set forth texts to

---

[36] This journal was published monthly from 1832–1842, but it did not run continuously. In 1836 Scott's *The Gospel Restored* was offered instead. In 1837 Scott published *The Christian* jointly with John T. Johnson.

[37] John T. Pressly, *Lectures on the Nature, Subjects and Mode of Christian Baptism* (Pittsburgh: A. Janes, 1841).

[38] Scott, *The Evangelist* (1 May 1841): p. 252; (1 December 1841): p. 275; (1 January, 1842): p. 9.

establish this case. Pressly had offered no biblical passages in support of infant baptism, only the inferences drawn from the analogy with infant inclusion in the Mosaic covenant. What Pressly overlooked, Scott suggested, was that circumcision was explicitly commanded in the Old Testament and that no such comparable command for infant baptism existed in the New Testament.[39] In the second installment Scott expressed his position explicitly:

> Now touching the baptism of children, not only there is not any of this plainness and particularly respecting it — not only is the observance of it not enforced by solemn sanctions—but it is absolutely not at all commanded, or even once named in all the sacred writings which, as Protestants, we have embraced as the rule of both our faith and practice.[40]

The church, Scott argued, as contrasted with the Abrahamic and Mosaic eras had a "new principle of membership." As biblical warrant for this claim, Scott cited Jeremiah 31, Hebrews 8, and John 6:45, passages treating the new Christian dispensation in which children would be taught God's ways. While a new relationship of humans with God is declared in these texts, these statements are never specifically related to conversion or baptism in the text themselves and therefore come under the strictures Scott himself directed toward Pressly. Scott accused Pressly of citing scriptures which applied only through inference and not directly. This approach Scott designated "reasoning instead of Scripture."[41] Scott's main argument, however, depended upon the declaration, "Baptism in connection with faith is commanded on pain of condemnation, but baptism without faith is not commanded at all."

Scott also addressed Pressly's position with respect to the mode of baptism, whether it should be by immersion, pouring, or sprinkling. Pressly, he pointed out, argued that "baptism" was employed by ancient non-Christian authors to convey dipping or plunging. Pressly further alleged that on many occasions this mode seems more possible than immersion, for example, the multitude baptized in Jerusalem on Pentecost, and the baptism of the Philippian jailer. Furthermore, Pressly declared inconclusive the instances of

---

[39]Scott, *The Evangelist* (1 May 1841): p. 108

[40]Ibid. (1 September 1841): p. 194.

[41]Ibid., p. 195.

the Ethiopian going down in the water, or Paul's phrase, "buried with him in baptism." While these might imply immersion, they by no means limited baptism to this mode.

Interestingly, in his first counter argument, Scott depended upon clear examples of immersion in the "ancient Latin Church down to the thirteenth century, and of the Greek Church down to the present day."[42] To these he added the testimonies of Luther, Calvin, Beza, Vitringa, Wall, Mead, Salmasius, and many others. The change to pouring and sprinkling, he declared, occurred in the days of Charlemagne in the eighth century. It was not until 1311 at the Council of Ravenna, however, that sprinkling was declared acceptable except in special cases. Scott then declared, "Calvin and the Protestant reformers owe sprinkling, then, to Rome; Knox and the Scotch Presbyterians owe it to Calvin; the English to the Scotch; and we Americans, to the English."[43] Rather the church, he contended, should depend on the authority of Peter as expressed in Acts 2:38. All discussion on baptism in the New Testament, Scott argued, involved adults and never focused on any aspect of introducing children into the church.

The apostolic appeal for people to be baptized was always directed toward sinners. It is impossible to plead with infants. Infants can understand none of the obligations required by baptism. Furthermore, infants are not pardoned in baptism—a conclusion, however, with which Pressly would not have agreed. Preaching, declared Scott, consists of declaring what God has done and calling the sinner to repentance. Infants can neither understand the first, nor do the latter. Scott next set forth the detailed testimonies of some ninety churchmen; most of these statements were written by British non-conformists, all ninety of whom claimed the necessity for a "plea for duty accompanying the proclamation of the gospel..."[44] Preaching of the duty to be baptized could not be directed toward infants.

Scott also cited the instances in the New Testament where persons received a call to duty. He considered these instances to be documentary evidences from which an induction or generalization could be drawn. Jesus called for repentance; Scott cited various examples. John the Baptist likewise elicited repentance, as did also Peter and Paul. Since these leaders pleaded for repentance and faith, so also must have the rest of the apostles. In addition, all

---

[42]Ibid., p. 196.
[43]Ibid., p. 196.
[44]Ibid., p. 205.

of these early leaders, in turn, called for baptism and the forgiveness of sins. The New Testament way therefore could not apply to infants:

> The ordinance, then is for the remission of sins, past sins. God had joined these two things together. And I do not argue that he who administers the rite to an infant puts them asunder, for every body knows that he does, an infant having no past sins to be forgiven; but I do affirm that the man who preaches repentance to an unconverted person whom he has sprinkled, cannot possibly preach remission to him as the apostles preached it. He cannot say with the apostle, "Be baptized for the remission of sins."[45]

From Acts 2:38 Scott furthered argued that baptism is followed by the gift of the Holy Spirit in this order, "conversion—baptism—pardon—the Holy Spirit."[46] Jesus blessed children and they will receive additional blessings when they attain remission of sins, but only when they believe the gospel and repent.[47] Scott ended this discourse with a plea for serious consideration of his argument, especially in view of the impending return of the Lord Jesus Christ.

In this polemical piece of writing, unlike his longer writings, Scott mostly ignored the Old Testament. His references and citations were mostly to the New Testament, especially to the gospels and Romans. Perhaps surprisingly, his one reference to Acts was Acts 2:38. Almost all of Scott's citations of scripture were to supply textual evidence for his declarations and arguments. In this case, he did not set out any embellished narratives, nor expand upon typologies. While he gave the testimony of authorities for proclamation and baptism, he did not bring to bear any commentators on the passages he cited.

The Divine Designs for History

Walter Scott clearly envisioned all history as the arena in which God achieves divine purpose. There are, however, two tiers, an inner and an outer, to history and to God's power within history. As Scott stated it:

> However varied, there are but two classes of sovereign power namely:

[45]Ibid., p. 207.
[46]Ibid., p. 210.
[47]Ibid., p. 212.

> The inner and the outer,
> or the spiritual and the political.
>
> The political is outward and secular, taking cognizance only of actions; the spiritual is inner and religious, taking cognizance also of thoughts. Israel was nationalized with these two classes of sovereign power, being personally and politically responsible to Moses, their civil ruler; and in their consciences subject to Aaron, as God's high priest, the head of the religious department.[48]

Scott believed the key to understanding the meaning of history could be revealed by understanding God's activity within history. Based upon his understanding that God worked within history to achieve divine purpose, Scott divided history into sacred ages by giving attention to the working out of God's purposes. Scott's designations for these sacred ages, for the biblical period, are as follows:

The Adamic or Antediluvian Age
The Noahitic or Patriarchal Age
The Mosaic Age, or Age of Organized Religion
John's or the Baptistic Age[49]
The Christian Age

Like most Protestants of his time, Scott divided post-biblical Christianity into eras. So he wrote: "The history of christianity, from Christ to the Millennium, may be divided into three parts, *Primitive Christianity*, the *Apostacy* and the *Reformation*."[50] He located the beginnings of the Reformation in the fourteenth century with Wycliffe and Hus. From the sixteenth century Scott mentioned Luther, Calvin, Knox, and Wesley. It was not until Scott's own time, however, that the Reformation had moved in the desired direction of restoration. Employing the metaphor of ships battling in a harbor, Scott identified the following developments, while subdividing some of the categories in much more detail:

Babylon, the "Mother of Harlots," that is, the Roman Catholic Church
The Eastern Orthodox

---

[48]Walter Scott, *The Messiahship*, p. 89.
[49]Ibid., p. 142.
[50]Scott, *The Evangelist* (2 January 1832): p. 19.

The Reformation
The Presbyterian
The Covenanters, that is, the Haldanean Scottish Baptists
The "Christians," that is, the O'Kelly, Jones-Smith, Stone people
The Restoration, that is, the Thomas and Alexander Campbell, Scott people.[51]

He was therefore not reticent in understanding history since the biblical period as an arena in which God continued to work out divine purposes. All of history was leading into the great contemporary movement, led by the Campbells and by Scott. And Scott believed the successes heralded by the beginning of this "restoration" led to the conclusion that the millennium would soon break into history.

From his earliest years of publication, Scott heralded the millennium. But he did not have a specific and well-defined version of it, contrary to the typical and very specific twentieth-century premillennial versions. From his writings, however, it is clear he believed, especially based upon his understanding of Daniel, that it was possible to predict the time of the millennium. And he believed that time was rapidly approaching. In the excitement created by William Miller (1782–1849), Scott wrote considerably on the subject even though he was not convinced of Miller's specific dating.[52] He later switched from a premillennialist view to a postmillennialist view—from the view that Christ would come to earth to launch the millennium (premillennialism) to the position shared by Alexander Campbell that the millennium would soon commence, but that Christ would not return until the end of a thousand years (postmillennialism), at which time history would end.[53] He therefore persisted in the view that history, as set forth in the Bible, is real history from beginning to end.

A statement written in 1832 indicates Scott's approach and his manner of employing the scripture so as to determine the time frame:

> In regard to the commencement of the Millennium, the year two thousand is probably to be fixed upon as its proper date. This is an old and perhaps correct idea derived

[51]Ibid. (1 April 1833): pp. 88–93
[52]Ibid. (1 December 1841): p. 277.
[53]Ibid. (4 June 1832): p. 121.

> from the fact, that in perfecting the material creation it pleased Almighty God, our heavenly Father, to allot to himself six spaces or days, and on the seventh to rest from all the works which he had made. Analogous to this, the true religion has been in a state of progression for nearly six thousand years, and it is most probable, all things considered, that the church will complete this number before she enters upon the enjoyment of that thousand years or millennium, which in this view of the matter, has been styled the Sabbatical Millennium...In unison with this, it has been observed: there were two thousand years before the calling of Abraham; two thousand from that time to the coming of the Messiah, and two thousand more under the Gospel which will most likely introduce the millennium. Again, the six thousand has been divided in the following manner: Solomon opened his temple at Jerusalem at the close of the third Millennium, and as his temple is conceived to be typical of that glorious state of things of which we are discoursing, let analogy number three thousand years from the time of the dedication, and it will bring us to the end of the year of our Lord two thousand, or to the year of the world six thousand, for the dedication of that splendid temple of things signified by the Millennium; but whether this calculation be correct or not, it is incontrovertible from the prophecies, from facts, and from the signs of the times, that we are fast approaching that eventful period when wickedness, and those who are guilty of it, shall speedily come to an end.[54]

As to political or outer ages, Scott also clearly located these within scripture. From the book of Daniel he held the succeeding empires to be the Assyrian Empire, the Medo-Persian, the Grecian, and the Roman. Those after the biblical period were the Gothic Kingdoms, the Papal Kingdom, and the Kingdom of God,[55] the last being the kingdom arriving at the millennium.

> This is the last empire the world will ever behold. It will, like those empires that have preceded it, be double, and embrace an inner and an outer, a political and a spiritual

[54]Ibid. (4 June 1832): p. 121.
[55]Scott, *The Messiahship*, 49.

> government—the former in the hands of God's saints, and the latter in the hands of his Son.[56]

In the time of the millennium, the earthly governments that are messianic will continue, and include Great Britain and the United States. This perspective led to the belief, shared by many Protestants of the time, that God possessed a great preference for the Anglo-Saxon race. God preferred the British and American governments over all the governments of the world. Once again Scott believed these delineations were revealed in scripture.

> These new governments, which we shall call Messianic or Christian governments, were to be created by Christianity in its progress throughout the world, and were to be great organic ensigns or standards lifted up upon the mountains, or in the midst of the nations declaring to all the world beside, that the great light who was to come into the world had come, and now calls the obedience of all nations a second time, or pain of being broken to pieces. Some of the nations it would seem will hear and admit in them the free circulation of the Gospel. This is what is signified by the Apocalyptic saying—"And there were great voices in heaven saying, The kingdoms of this world are become kingdoms of our Lord, even of his Messiah, and he shall reign forever and ever."— Rev. 11:15.

In regard to Great Britain, Scott wrote:

> Among the Christian governments of the old world—among the organic standards of Messiah—none unfurls a broader and more glorious banner than Great Britain. What hope would we have of improvement, were *she* struck from the map of nations? Who but she is making headway against corrupted Christianity and Mahometism, idolatry, and tyranny? Who but she keeps in check the northern and southern despotisms, Russia and France? Who, like her, is enkindling the beacon fires of a Christian civilization on all the high places and standpoints of the world? Who but she by her colonies is creating new nations and a new world? She is the great mother of nations. But for her,

[56]Ibid., p. 118.

> idolatry should maintain its ancient immobility forever, and but for her, Catholicism would lead all Europe backward five hundred years to the dark ages and the days of Saint Gregory.[57]

But Scott expected even more of The United States.

> But admitting the greatness and glory of the English Ensign, it is perhaps only in America, in the United States, that we see the banner of human rights floating highest, and its billowy foldings made most resplendent by the light of the Sun of Righteousness. In Great Britain and the United States we have before us, one in the new and one in the old world, the most illustrious proofs that the Messiah who was to come is come, and that the better order of things indicated in the prophets is inaugurated in these two governments at least. In America we have a new world, a new people, a new government, and in Washington a new hero. Can the symbols and imagery of the prophets then ever be more literally realized? Can the "new heavens and the new earth," that is the new government and the new people of prophesy, ever be more evidently verified than by a case in which we have a new world, a new people, and new government and a new hero? Impossible. Seeing then, that these two governments arose out of our common Christianity, let us cherish the blessed thought that if, with their population of fifty millions, they can not be styled the church, yet they are at least the state or civilization which the church was, after the lapse of ages of suffering, to create, and which, by their political ameliorations as standard-bearers of the "army of the faith," were to prove to the ends of the earth, that "he who was to come is come."
>
> "All ye inhabitants of the world and dwellers on the earth see ye when he lifteth up an ensign upon the mountains." Isa. 18:3.[58]

---

[57]Ibid., p. 297.
[58]Ibid., p. 298.

The question now remains: how did Scott use the Bible in order to support his conclusions about the unfolding of sacred and secular history? The narrative portion of the Bible played a big role, but often through an interpretation based upon an understanding of the importance of types and antitypes. Therefore, it is important to address briefly Scott's typological hermeneutics. He set out his type/antitype presuppositions as follows:

> Revealed religion may be divided into the shadow and the substantive, the typical and the antitypical, or the things of the Old Testament and those of the New—the former extending from Adam to Christ, and the latter from Christ to the resurrection of the dead. In these two parts of the system respectively, Adam and Christ stand to each other in the relation of type and antitype; for this we have the authority of Scripture.
>
> 1. A type defined—It must be ordained by the author.
>
> 2. It must be ground on a matter of fact in the antitype.
>
> 3. It must foreshadow that fact.

This is substantially the definition of a type as given by Horn. The typology of scripture is founded on resemblance; symbol on difference. [59]

In a vision of how this applied to the Bible as a whole, Scott wrote:

> Restricting our researches to the Bible, we find it divided into two parts, namely, the Old Testament and the New—or the Jewish and the Christian Scriptures—the former the shadow, the latter the substance—the first typical, the second antitypical. These interact harmoniously with each other, and the whole is perfectly consistent, with itself.
>
> Revelation is the boundary of both; the law and the gospel are both of God, but the former was the shadow cast before the latter; Adam, Noah, Melchisedek, Moses,

[59]Ibid., p. 34.

> Aaron, the Tabernacle, and the Kingdom were but figures of the things of our religion.[60]

Scott's presentation of Moses as a type for Christianity provides an example:

Moses as a Type/Antitype

1. The Redeemer: Moses Messiah
2. TheRedeemed: Israel unorganized Christians Unorganized
3. The Rescue or Transition: Cloud and Sea Water and Spirit
4. Their Civil and Religious Organization: The same
5. Their Wilderness State: Their state in the world
6. Their Hope of Canaan: Their hope in heaven[61]

About the type/antitype approach, Hans W. Frei, the cult hero of Yale Divinity School's Post-Modernism, perceptively wrote:

> Without loss of its own literal meaning or specific temporal reference, an earlier story (or occurrence) was a figure of a later one. The customary use of figuration was to show that Old Testament persons, events, and prophecies were fulfilled in the New Testament. It was a way of turning the variety of biblical books into a single, unitary canon, one that embraced in particular the differences between Old and New Testaments.[62]

Frei's statement may express the position of Scott more than at first meets the eye. One wonders why Scott, so interested in New Testament Christianity, spent so much time explicating the Old Testament. The answer is that he thought that the movement from type to antitype established the veracity of the biblical faith. For this reason he gave little emphasis to the obsolete features of the types. In fact, he believed that the antitype enhanced the significance of the type rather than downgrading it.

---

[60]Ibid., p. 10.

[61]Ibid., p. 82.

[62]Hans W. Frei, *The Eclipse of Biblical Narrative* (New Haven: Yale University Press, 1974), p. 2.

> If the reader will devote a few moments to the contemplation of the types which I have handled; if he will look at Adam, Noah, Melchizedek, Moses, Aaron, Israel, and the tabernacle successively in connection with the persons and things which they represent, he will see that the high places of the ancient oracles shine with an evangelical luminousness which, without the antitypical religion of christianity, they could not possibly possess; and he will read with ease and pleasure under the splendor of the sun of righteousness all the grand doctrines of our religion. The Old Testament will in this way be transfigured into the New, and withal offer to him the most evident tokens, not only of God's knowledge of the future, but all of his great and unsearchable wisdom and providence toward us who believe, in regard to the past in causing it to minister to the future—the shadow to the substance—the type to the antitype, Adam, Noah, Melchizedek, Moses, Aaron, Israel, and the tabernacle to Christ and christianity.[63]

Scott's use of biblical narrative may be clarified even further by examining his comments on "The Resurrection of Christ" in *The Messiahship*. Scott contended that the resurrection was anticipated in the Old Testament. "In the work of Adam and the work of Christ we have the genesis and regenesis—the generative and regenerative elements of the revealed system. The key to the truth and authority of the whole is the resurrection of the Messiah."[64] Scott then proceeded to set out what he designated as the reports about the resurrection. He presented two reports from the Old Testament, "Isaiah's Report" and "David's Report." In these cases, Scott cited a few texts from each. But when he turned to the New Testament he mostly quoted from the narratives, first the Acts, which he labeled "Peter's Report," then Matthew, Mark, Luke, and John. Next he presented Paul's report which consisted of Paul's speech before Agrippa in Acts, then "Christ's Report" which consisted mostly of quotations from the Gospel of John and Revelation.[65] Scott elaborated little upon these biblical narratives. He concluded by declaring that conviction about the resurrection of Christ results from reading the narratives of the witnesses. Scott did not

---

[63]Scott, *The Messiahship*, pp. 106, 107.
[64]Ibid., p. 186.
[65]Ibid., pp. 184–198.

entertain the notion that these biblical witnesses might be questioned as to whether their reports accurately reflected the events as they occurred.

> The Messiahship of Jesus is in reality the deduction of a resplendent truth from an induction of stupendous facts, objective facts made good to us by testimony. So that in our religion facts are the heralds of reason and reason the herald of faith.[66]

Conclusions

Walter Scott viewed the Bible and its interpretation much like his Scottish contemporaries. His approaches were also widely accepted in America. He consulted standard British authors of the time, but ventured little into cutting edge German biblical scholarship. His biblical scholarship was surprisingly much focused on biblical narratives and more on the Old Testament than one might suspect for one who was committed to restoring the ancient order and gospel of the New Testament church. This commitment was made possible through his type/antitype hermeneutics. For Scott the Bible clearly has a story line running from Genesis through Revelation. He did not concern himself much with the language and grammar of the Bible. He was especially concerned with the historical character of the biblical materials, but he did not utilize the scholars, to any extent, who set out to establish historical authenticity.

Scott's legacy remains in the movement of which he was a founder, more in some parts than others.[67] Especially still observable within the movement, but now eroding, is the hegemony of reason when interpreting the Bible and the propensity to set out schemata. But because in most wings of the movement an amillennial posture has been assumed, few any longer share Scott's conviction that biblical materials provide historical clues, not only for the past, but also for the present and future. While one may question whether it is possible by reading the Bible to declare tomorrow's headlines today, still, the position of the modern

---

[66]Ibid., p. 202.

[67]Mention should be made of M. Eugene Boring, *Disciples and the Bible: A History of Disciples Biblical Interpretation in North America* (St. Louis: Chalice Press, 1997), especially pp. 30–51. Professor Boring provided me with a copy of the manuscript, which included a discussion of Walter Scott and from which I benefited.

movement has seemed to stifle the biblical vision that God continues to be active in human affairs and is leading history to a divine and desired conclusion. Scott believed wholeheartedly in that biblical vision.

So I conclude in the modus operandi of the one whose life is celebrated in these pages: Walter Scott (1796–1861), a creator, a maker of schemata, an untiring Bible student, a consummate evangelist, a committed believer, a significant ancestor.

CHAPTER FIVE

"Stupendous Facts": Walter Scott's Primitivist Spirituality

T. Dwight Bozeman

Within the Restoration Movement of the nineteenth century, what did the founders' program of recovery and reduction entail for *praxis pietatis* (the practice of piety)? How did the determination of Stoneites, Campbellites, or other "Christians" to cast aside human inventions and recover biblical ways alter the traditions of Protestant Reformed spirituality in which most of the founders had been bred? The present essay provides an initial approach to this question by way of a case study. Focused upon Walter Scott (1796–1861), a major figure in the movement from the later 1820s until the Civil War, it explores the bearing of his stringent restorationist program upon his understanding of the saints' affective and devotional relation to God.[1]

Scott is a suitable choice for the study because, so he believed, recovery of the exact apostolic doctrine of redemption was his

[1]For a similar study, see D. Newell Williams, "The Gospel as the Power of God to Salvation: Alexander Campbell and Experimental Religion," in James M. Seale, ed., *Lectures in Honor of the Alexander Campbell Bicentennial*, 1788–1988 (Nashville: Disciples of Christ Historical Society, 1988), pp. 127–148.

distinctive contribution. In *The Gospel Restored* (1836) he highlighted that doctrine as the third and culminating element of the Restoration Movement: first, Thomas Campbell and others had put forth the Bible as the exclusive authority for Christian faith and practice; second, Alexander Campbell had isolated in sacred writ the "Apostolic Order" of church organization; and finally Scott himself had restored the True Gospel.[2] Compressed into his famous six principles, the True Gospel was the message of "Faith, Repentance, Baptism, Remission of Sins, the Holy Spirit, and the Resurrection…"[3] These essentials, in this exact order, defined the biblical plan of redemption; they marked "the way, and the only way into the kingdom…"[4] And they laid the basis for a diminished, but still vital, spirituality.

Several features of Scott's theology operated to reduce both the range and the relative importance of spirituality. First, and by explicit design, the True Gospel drastically trimmed the number of historic doctrines of redemption. Scott pointedly discarded, for instance, the great Reformed concept of predestination and its large battery of associated ideas. And in rough proportion as it constricted historic soterial teaching, so the gospel according to Walter Scott supplied fewer resources and incentives to spirituality. Just as he undid much of the work of the long-lived scholastic period in Reformed theology, so he dismantled—or bitingly ignored—most of the concerns of the great devotional renaissance which had arisen both in Catholic and Protestant sectors throughout Europe and Britain from the later sixteenth century, and had done much to form the traditions of piety in the Scots and English Reformed traditions with which Scott was most familiar.

What students of historic Protestant spirituality may find most striking in his work is the simple disappearance of most of the familiar landmarks of that spirituality. To take but a few examples from the long-lived Reformed *praxis pietatis*, Scott ignored or marginalized the "spiritual exercises" of preparation for conversion: fasting, systematic introspection, the "watch" over temptations, meditation, spiritual diaries, the catalogue of sins, the quest for "signs and evidences" of a safe estate before God, or daily

[2]Walter Scott, *The Gospel Restored. A Discourse of the True Gospel of Jesus Christ, in which the Facts, Principles, Duties, and Priviliges* [sic] *of Christianity are Arranged, Defined, and Discussed,…*[hereafter *GR*] (Cincinnati, 1836), pp. v–vi.

[3]*The Evangelist* (2 January 1832): p. 9.

[4]Ibid.(4 June 1832): p. 124.

devotional schedules.[5] He devoted relatively little attention to spirituality and made no effort to formulate a distinctive practice of piety for his new reformation.

Second, Scott designed his True Gospel partly as a critique of the exuberant and emotion laden revivalism of the Second Great Awakening and its espousal of "the invention named '*Experimental Religion*.'"[6] "Experimental" in this context meant felt, experienced, and thus it honored human feelings as a manifestation and index of true faith and standing before God. Yet all of this Scott brusquely cast aside. Like the older spiritual exercises, experimental religion lacked biblical warrant; but more, in his estimate it had made Christianity "the mere vehicle of feelings" and ephemeral "bursts of enthusiasm" at the expense of its more rational and stable qualities.[7] In phrases such as these, Scott revealed affinities with the resurgent churchly reaction of the period against the revival system and its emphasis upon individual and subjective experience.

Like High Church Episcopalians, confessional Lutherans, or the Mercersburg theologians, he moved to downplay the subjective and accent anew the objective aspects of the faith. By the 1820s it was time to summon the faithful away from "their own frames and feelings" (notoriously "variant and fugitive") and to fix their attention upon the objective, factual reality of the Bible and the apostolic sacraments. Whereas in popular evangelical faith the core doctrine of the pardon of sin had come to rest upon feeling and had "no tangible, no positive form whatever," Scott's proudest contribution to the Restoration Movement was his rediscovery that pardon is tied apostolically to the rite of adult baptism. Nothing could better impart a solid "ordinancial and positive shape" to the reality of forgiveness, or apply a more potent antidote to revivalism's subjective vagueness.[8] Thus did "feeling," an

---

[5]Charles E. Hambrick-Stowe, *The Practice of Piety: Puritan Devotional Disciplines in Seventeenth-Century New England* (Chapel Hill, 1982) offers one avenue of approach to the devotional renaissance and traditional Reformed spirituality. Scott did advocate a regular hour-long ritual of morning prayer. Scott, "Morning Prayer," *The Protestant Unionist* (25 September, 1844): p. 1. On prayer, see also Scott, "Prayer," *The Protestant Unionist* (27 November, 1844): 17.

[6]*The Evangelist* (2 September 1833): p. 206.

[7]Ibid., p. 206.

[8]Scott, *GR*, pp. 300, 418, 302. For "resurgent churchly traditions" in the period, see H. Shelton Smith, Robert T. Handy, and Lefferts A. Loetscher, *American Christianity: An Historical Interpretation with Representative Documents*, 2 vols. (New York: Scribners, 1963): 2, pp. 66–118. The authors do not include the Restoration Movement under this rubric.

obviously central element in piety, become problematic in Scott's thought.

Third, and similarly, a favorite target of Scott's polemic, directed both against the older Protestant theology and experimental religiosity, was the claim that "the Holy Spirit is necessary to produce faith." It was a first axiom of the True Gospel that faith is a rational act of conviction and choice well within human capacity; wherefore all presumed "special operations" of the Holy Spirit before faith are both illusory and superfluous. In the belief, thus, that "the Spirit is not granted to change the heart, but in the Christian system is given to a man because his heart is already changed by the [rational] belief of the truth," Scott at once undercut devotional interest in the older preparatory and penitential exercises prior to faith and diluted the orthodox sense of faith as divine embrace and transformation.[9]

Fourth, Scott understood and presented the True Gospel, which in his lexicon comprised Christianity's basic religious message, essentially as an instrument of evangelism. It was directed more to "converting the world" than to personal or ecclesiastical nurture. In light of the expansive, energetically proselytizing state of the New Reformation in the 1820s and 1830s, it was surely no accident that the first five of his six principles (faith, repentance, baptism, pardon of sins, endowment with the Spirit) described sinful and doomed humanity's *initial* entry into the kingdom of redemption. So it was, too, that *The Gospel Restored*, Scott's compendious summary of "the facts, principles, duties, and priviliges [*sic*] of Christianity," was essentially a review of humankind's need for redemption followed by discussions of Christ's messianic work and its application to the lives of men and women through the six principles. His relatively few and scattered discussions of Christian nurture focused upon questions of "good order" and "the media of worship" and showed but moderate interest in individual or communal expressions of piety. For the most part, he relegated the means "to keep [baptized and Spirit-endowed persons] Christians" to ecclesiology and left them to Alexander Campbell and others to unfold.[10]

---

[9]*The Evangelist* (5 February 1832): pp. 28, 27; Scott, *GR*, p. 490.

[10]Ibid. (7 January 1833): 16; *GR*, title page; *The Evangelist* (April 1835): p. 88. See also ibid.: "All the matters of Christianity, as a popular institution, may be divided into those of faith and those of order; or they are either evangelical, or ecclesiastical. The evangelical are those which constitute the good news or gospel which is intended to make men Christians. The ecclesiastical are those which ordain good order and are intended as the media of Christian worship; for to make men Christians and to keep them Christians is the amount of the entire institution."

In other ways, too, Scott's six principle gospel reduced incentives to the cultivation of piety. For centuries the great warfare of the soul with flesh, world, and devil had supplied the principal subject matter of pious meditation and exercise. Even in Protestant contexts in which the "Lutheran" theme of *sola gratia, sola fide* predominated (and there were many in which this was not the case), an ongoing, strenuous struggle against temptation and sin was assumed as a normal routine of the Christian life. In Scott's world of thought, however, the emphasis shifted. As he summarized the matter in *Gospel Restored*, "faith, repentance, baptism, remission, the Holy Spirit, and the resurrection cancel severally the love, the practice, the state, the guilt, the power, and the punishment of sin..."[11]

The language of "cancellation," enhanced by Scott's assumption of the objective reality and effect of the gospel and sacraments, projected a view of the Christian life in which sin plays a relatively unproblematic part. After baptism, for example, which Scott defined as the vehicle of an immediate and total pardon of all past faults, there was no need to "appease an awakened conscience by the mortifications of the cloister, the severities of penance, or the voluntary humilities of an austere devotion: for [the] Lord has borne [the sinner's] griefs and carried his sorrows, and through him he has redemption, *even the forgiveness of sins*."[12]

And as to sins committed and guilt accrued after baptism,this too posed no grave concern for Scott, for he assumed that the personal repentance which preceded baptism, and the endowment with the Spirit which accompanied it, effectively tamed the self, removing in large measure the love and power of sin. In Scott's own words: "The Christian religion...put[s] all its converts into immediate possession of...the *spirit* of holiness" and they act accordingly. Here was a far more optimistic estimate of what redemption does to a man or woman than could be found in any classical Catholic or Protestant creed, and it left little ground for an elaborate penitential piety of the traditional sort.[13] This is all the more true, when we recall that the construction and maintenance of

---

[11]*GR*, p. 94. See also *The Evangelist* (5 November 1832): p. 243.

[12]*The Evangelist* (7 January 1833): pp. 19–20. See also *GR*, p. 302: "He, who is baptized on a true and living faith in the blood of Christ, is no longer troubled with his former or past sins."

[13]*The Evangelist* (4 June 1832): p. 135. See also *GR*, p. 87: After baptism and the reception of the Spirit, "love shall supercede [*sic*] hatred, gentleness, anger and meekness, revenge, and all the graces of God's Spirit shall be transferred to the human heart again."

rigorous inward controls was the primary objective of the older spiritual exercises.

Yet, to review the downsizing effects of restoration upon piety is not to tell the whole story, and, certainly, to assume that Scott's aim was to nullify devotion in every traditional sense would be a serious mistake; for each of the six principles describes a unit of experience in which the self is brought under the sway of a wonder-working power which excites and uplifts the emotions and stimulates devotional activity. Serious consideration of the gospel and of Christ its founder has "the power," in Scott's words, "of affecting the mind and of changing its condition both intellectually and morally, both in regard to its view and feelings." The act of faith, for instance, releases supernatural "illuminations" into the mind; these "influence the affections, [and change]...the heart," and repentance is but a name for that change.

Further, were not both repentance and pardon detoxifying processes that make it possible for the Spirit in all his purity to "descend" into the soul? And does not the Spirit within impart a "superhuman strength" to the soul that in turn, stirs emotions that no earthly scenes or powers could evoke, including "joy, love, peace, gentleness, and every divine grace"?[14] As a transcendental and deeply affecting message from God to humankind, it was therefore not only proper but essential that the gospel, in Scott's express phrase, "be made a business of devotional consideration and prayer."[15]

High among the emotions and graces that Scott praised stood a centuries old, definitive theme of Augustinian piety: love. For the present purpose, it is worthy of note that Scott occasionally singled out this grace, telling his audiences that "the love of God in Christ" imbues the receptive soul with a reciprocal "filial disposition towards God," or that the "belief and hope in what God has done and promised operate to give birth to *love*" which "terminates on the Deity."[16] For all his primitivist's dismissal of the older, and certainly the medieval, traditions of Christianity, Scott found

[14]Scott, *GR*, pp. 316, 256, 409, 412. See also ibid., 87, 295; and Scott, *The Messiahship, or Great Demonstration, Written for the Union of Christians, on Christian Principles, as Plead for in the Current Reformation* (Cincinnati, 1859), p. 44. Cf. D. Newell Williams' argument that Alexander Campbell "taught the reality and desirability of personal religious experience, while rejecting the standard nineteenth century evangelical views of how that experience is obtained." Williams, "The Gospel as the Power of God to Salvation," in Seale, ed., *Lectures in Honor of the Alexander Campbell Bicentennial*, p. 128.

[15]*The Evangelist* (6 November 1833): p. 259, "Institution."

[16]Scott, *GR*, p. 295; *The Evangelist* (1 January 1835): p. 27. See also Scott, *GR*, p. 220.

remaining threads of value in historic spirituality. Only thus can we explain the remarkable passage in *Gospel Restored* in which he added the names of Saint Augustine, Saint Bernard, Saint Thomas á Kempis, and Pico della Mirandola—the latter three standing squarely in the Augustinian tradition of neoplatonic piety—to a rollcall of saints who had grasped the gospel's "celestial and efficacious power [to] inflam[e] the soul with divine fear and love."[17]

In light of Scott's special theological program, however, love, fear, joy, and other reverential emotions required careful, restrictive focusing. That the means of redemption are conveyed through scripture alone was the root principle of the Restoration Movement, and the endeavor to "mount up the stream of Christian history to its [biblical] source and...drink of the waters as they flowed purely from the great fountain of life, at the beginning" had potent implications for spirituality as well as for theology and ecclesiology. It tended both to magnify the interest and prestige of biblical narratives beyond the Protestant average and to find in them the exclusive objects of devotion. Biblical scenes, primal and pure, were by definition sublime and therefore deeply affecting; and often enough Scott's telling of the primitive stories radiated devotional feeling. "Behold," he could demand,

> the symbol of divine mercy! the ark, riding upon a world of waters—a sea without a shore! who is its inmate?—whence is he? and whither does he go[?] It is the child of faith—the patriarch Noah; he escapes from the world that had sinned— The foundations of the great deep have been broken up—the windows of heaven have been opened, and the world is dissolved—[18]

and much more of the same.

Scott's perception of primitive events as uniquely sublime and emotionally potent casts light upon another well-known side of his theology: his conception of faith as an intellectual persuasion, generated not by inward motions of the Spirit but by a natural and rational process. As impressed as any mainstream theologian with contemporary canons of scientific method, he defined faith as

---

[17]Scott, *GR*, pp. 223–224. Scott quoted the references to Augustine, Bernard, á Kempis and Mirandola from a secondary source, but did so with obvious approval.

[18]Scott, *GR*, pp. 185, 263–264. See also the discussion of Enoch and Moses in ibid., pp. 264, 267.

intellectual assent based upon observation of the miracles and other empirical "evidences" or "proofs" which accompany the central biblical truths. Obviously this conception drew upon Enlightenment sources, and some scholars have emphasized its rationalistic and to some degree mechanistic tendencies.[19] Such tendencies are undeniably present. To ground religious faith in empirical proof, on the grounds that "we must believe what is proved" by evidence, comes close to equating faith with wholly rational and secular processes of induction. It seems to allow no categorical difference between, say, belief that Jesus was the Messiah and belief in gravity.[20] Yet the man who seemed to derive faith mechanically from evidence was the same man who responded with scarcely scientific rapture to the biblical narratives which contained the relevant "evidence."

In Scott's scheme of things, the principal truth of the gospel to be proven was the Messiahship of Jesus Christ, and that was demonstrated by an array of evidences, among which Jesus' miracles were the most immediate and striking. Yet in Scott's account it was perfectly clear that the evidential properties of miracles—and hence the basic meaning of "proof" itself—are unique. For miracles belong to a world of a higher order, to the biblical times suffused with supernatural presence and power and endowed with the special prestige that restorationist theologies assign to the normative time. All the evidences by which Jesus "proved that he was the Christ" are embraced in that world; and they are, in a word, "marvelous." Certainly they share qualities with other kinds of evidence. Their sheer number and variety, for example, conduce to belief; but then so do the number and variety of falling bodies or chemical reactions observed by physical scientists. In the last analysis the miracles' convicting power rests upon other grounds entirely, upon their character as divine and primitive wonders. The Messiahship is proved by no everyday logic of evidence and inference but by "an induction of *stupendous* facts."[21]

Through those facts, furthermore, the Holy Spirit—the "great demonstrator"—speaks.[22] He does not, Scott hastened to say, speak

---

[19]See, e.g., William A. Gerrard III, "Walter Scott: Frontier Disciples Evangelist," unpub. Ph.D. diss., Emory University, 1990, pp. 163–165, 184, 187–188.

[20]*Christian Baptist*, 6, p. 243.

[21]Ibid., 1, p. 31; Scott, *Messiahship*, 202, emphasis mine. In ibid., p. 30, Scott drew attention to the "great" and "amazing" properties of miracles.

[22]Scott, "The Gospel Advocacy," *The Protestant Unionist* (15 January 1845): p. 45.

from within, for that would affirm the very inward "operations" of the deity prior to faith which he was at such pains to deny; but speaking from without and through the medium of miracles, he speaks powerfully to both mind and heart. "Listen," Scott could say, "to the Spirit speaking to you in the mouth of the Apostles and Prophets, and he will afford you abundant evidence by which you can believe..." It is evidence such as this, evidence framed in miracle and spoken by the deity, evidence of incomparable "magnitude,...sublimity, and benignity," that will finally "delight, astonish and instruct us" and thereby "carry irresistable [*sic*] conviction to the heart,..." Bearing only outward resemblance to the process of demonstration in philosophy or science, therefore, the impact of miracles upon the mind is as singular as the miracles themselves. It represents a highly specialized instance of "spiritual moral suasion."[23]

It was so with the apostles themselves, who "were so inspired by the strangeness and sublimity of the events which they were ordained to witness, that even in the presence of their enemies they cried out that 'we cannot but speak of the things which we have seen and heard.'"[24] Such words bore deep conviction, and what was that conviction but itself a kind of reverence, a state of wonder evoked by wonders, and a realization of their tremendous import for human welfare and fate? So the theory of evidences was not so merely rational or mechanistic after all, and Scott clearly knew that no ordinary logic of evidence could account for the faith of which he spoke. It was the fruit of a special, transcendental induction, itself a genuine wonder in the world and a spring of unearthly emotions, meditations, and prayers.

Always the sacred narratives, seen through primitivist lenses, supplied the materials of devotion, and indeed one of the most evocative passages in Scott's late study of *The Messiahship* (1859) gives a passionately devotional salute to scripture itself: "O Book of God! thou sacred temple! thou holy place! thou lightgiving, gold candlestick! thou gold incense altar! thou heavenly shewbread! thou cherubim-embroidered veil! thou shekinah in which the divinity is enshrined! thou Ark of the Covenant! thou new creation! thou

---

[23]*The Evangelist* (4 February 1833): p. 44; *Christian Baptist*, 1, p. 32; Scott, "The Gospel Advocacy," p. 45. See also *The Evangelist* (1 April 1833): p. 82: In the production of "religious belief, the proposition, the proof and the person submitting them, are all divine."

[24]Ibid. (2 September 1833): pp. 205–206.

tree of life,...! thou new Jerusalem, resplendent with gems and gold! thou Paradise of God,..."[25]

Nevertheless, Scott did not attach equal importance to all the passages of scripture. Like all biblical theologians he employed a canon within the canon which privileged certain narratives and themes over others. As easily could be determined by an inventory of his scriptural citations with respect to their frequency and degree of emphasis, his six-principle summary of the apostolic message called preferential attention to a small set of biblical texts and subjects. These cannot all be canvassed here, but we offer a sampler of two.

First, given Scott's conviction that belief in Jesus' Messiahship was the core of the Christian redemption, the "very sun of the spiritual system," it is no surprise that the Messiah also emerged as a central focus of his devotional interest.[26] Other heroic personages of the primitive time evoked rapturous expressions from him too, but he clearly found the highest evocative power in the one whom he affirmed as the Son of God and the world's Savior. Noah and Moses were mortals after all, but Christ was "transcendently excellent." He was himself the great "wonder of wonders," "heaven's last, best gift" to humankind. And as to his redeeming work, his voluntary incarnation and heroic self-sacrifice, "What solemn themes are these! [And] ought they not to be bathed 'in many tears' by him whose sacred office it is to announce them?"[27]

Many details of the Messiah's earthly and heavenly life stirred Scott to the quick. Thus, in a meditation in *The Evangelist* for 1833 that draws upon the famous and ancient strain of bridal mysticism in both Catholic and Protestant devotion, and which therefore stands in some tension with his desire to break with corrupting tradition, he spoke of the believer in Christ with silent reference to the portrayal of lovers in the Song of Songs:

> His Beloved is more than another Beloved, the chiefest among ten thousand, and his love is better than wine. To him, IMMANUEL is the source of supreme enjoyment, and the unfailing fountain of perennial delight. The draughts of pleasure which he receives from Him...are purer than

[25]Scott, *Messiahship*, p. 263. See also ibid., p. 269, and Scott, "The Bible," *The Protestant Unionist* (1 December 1847), p. 205.

[26]*Christian Baptist* 1, p. 111.

[27]*GR*, p. 221; Scott, *Messiahship*, p. 30; *The Evangelist* (2 April 1832): p. 90; Scott, *Messiahship*, p. 182.

> the streams of Lebanon...He loves to look off to Jesus, and to contemplate the object of his affections,

...and the like. Or again, in a meditation in *The Gospel Restored* that belongs to a long history of devotional rumination upon the Passion, he imagined himself in the Messiah's immensely affecting presence:

> Methinks I see the cross thrown down upon the ground, and the great substitute for man racked to the dimensions of its cursed limbs! Exhausted and forlorn, the hands that aye were filled with blessings and deeds of love and charity, are rudely seized by the ironhanded Roman, and nailed to the murderous wood; the feet, those feet that ever trod the path of peace, are spiked and barred to make the offering sure! Death! death! horrible in every shape! [28]

...and so on.

Likewise, it was that death, horrible in shape, that Scott made central to eucharistic meditation. His interpretation of the supper emphasized its memorial function, for it was precisely "in order to keep constantly in our minds the great facts of his death and second coming [that Christ]...instituted the supper." When, therefore, we attend to the rite, properly cleansed of impurifying additions to the original,

> our minds are led back to the sufferings and death of Jesus Christ for the sins of an apostate world; we can contemplate his agony in the garden, when he sweat[ed]...great drops of blood falling down to the ground; we see him arraigned at the bar of Pilate, and condemned to death, the first martyr to the truth of his religion; we see him nailed to the accursed tree, and through the Eternal Spirit offering himself without spot to God...[29]

Scott's devotional engagement with the Messiah extended into many other areas, into considerations of Christ's resurrected life and rule and the reappearance in the skies at the last judgment, for

---

[28]*The Evangelist* (7 January 1833): p. 18; *GR*, p. 404. Note also Scott's interest in Christ's "Transfiguration" as "a Daguerrotype, or...*tableau vivant*, of the resurrection state,...[which should] be the theme of our most devout meditation." Scott, *Messiahship*, p. 2.

[29]*The Evangelist* (1 September 1835): p. 218. See also Scott, *Messiahship*, p. 183.

instance; but the examples given above suggest that Scott's restorationist program gave rise to an emotionally striking spirituality, and that study of that spirituality illuminates many details of the Restoration Movement as he conceived it.[30]

A second prime focus of Scott's devotion, and one equally revealing of his canon within the canon, was the resurrected life in heaven. The scriptural evidence was sparse, but once a conspectus of heaven had been gathered from scattered passages, this "sixth principle" was breathtaking to behold. Then, when

> the whole church shall be gathered home, there will be seen in heaven [a] wonderful spectacle—the church glorified; filled with the Holy Spirit, into which she had been baptized: the Son at her head, by whom she has been redeemed; and God on his throne, by whom she has been glorified.[31]

As in this example, Scott's many praises of the heavenly life are far more esthetic than theological in spirit, and they reveal a remarkably full-blown devotional orientation to the afterlife. Consider, for instance, this effusion from *The Gospel Restored*:

> O, what boundless regions of glorious thought have been redeemed to man by the elevation of Jesus to the throne of God! Youth, immortal youth, beauty, loveliness, and eternal life, the kingly ornaments of wisdom, greatness, dignity, veneration, crowns, the imperial pomp of powers, virtues, dominations, principalities, thrones, the social glory of the general assembly and congregation of the heirs in heaven, of angels innumerable, spirits perfectly just, and God, and Christ the Mediator of the New Covenant: Hallelujah.

Or again, in *The Evangelist* for 1835 Scott published a letter to an acquaintance which expressed a moving

> desire to embrace you in heaven; and to stand with my hand clasped in yours, with all the saints, before the throne of the Most High...O, when shall we see God!...I have thought of the mount of deliverance. I have fancied the

[30]See, for example, *The Evangelist* (2 January 1832): p. 8; ibid. (2 April 1832): p. 90; ibid. (7 May 1832): pp. 102–103; ibid. (4 February 1833): pp. 43–44; *GR*, p. 221.

[31]Ibid. (4 February 1833): p. 36.

> great Shepherd reclining there, in the midst of his redeemed flock. I have imagined to myself the heavenly vales, and the stream of life issuing from the throne, and dispersing into myriads of branches and watering all the heavenly realms. Shall we see this great multitude which no man can number? Shall we see the Patriarchs? Shall we see the Prophets—and the apostles—and the saints and the martyrs...shall we see Jesus himself and his holy angels, and God the Father? Yes; if we overcome, Jesus says we shall sit down with him on his throne...[32]

A myriad of such expressions in Scott's work make clear that the sixth of his famous principles entailed a frank, powerfully felt, and meditative otherworldliness.

The Messiah and the heavenly fatherland—these were but two objects of pious desire and reflection in Scott's repertoire. A fuller account would note in particular how ardently and often he reviewed the stirring scenes of the first Pentecost in the second chapter of the Acts.[33]

To return, now, to the original question—what did Scott's program of recovery and reduction entail for *praxis pietatis*?—at least some elements of an answer now are evident. Indeed, the endeavor to ascend the stream of Christian history to the original time had fateful consequences for prevailing traditions of Protestant and Reformed spirituality. Rejecting the spasmodic emotionalism of nineteenth century revivals, redefining the inherited doctrine of the Spirit's stirring "operations" within the self before faith as an external and evidential process, the plan of restoration also swept away a vast litter of emotions and spiritual exercises that seemed to lack biblical warrant. From virtually any traditional standpoint within the Reformed mainstream, this must seem an impoverishing result. As a High Church Episcopalian or a Mercersburg theologian might say, it was as though Scott had brushed away a little dust, and the dust was preparation for conversion, or

---

[32]Scott, *GR*, p. 272; *The Evangelist* (1 September 1835): p. 207.

[33]No primitive scene was more crucial to the restorationist program as Scott constructed it. It not only clearly manifested every one of the six principles; it also demonstrated their truth with an outpouring of miraculous evidences second only to the miracles of Christ himself. It also marked the fateful moment in the apostolic history when the Holy Spirit was given to the church and thus was made available to baptized believers in post-apostolic time. See, e.g., *Christian Baptist* 1, pp. 135–137; Scott, *GR*, pp. 413–417, 535–536; *The Protestant Unionist* (9 December 1846), p. 2, and ibid. (13 January 1847): p. 27.

systematic meditation. Whisk and fasting and the many other ascetic rites by which generations had sought a greater likeness to God, all were gone. So, too, the place once held by careful introspection or the daily devotional schedule now stood empty. Whisk, spiritual diaries and journals; whisk, the catalogue of sins; whisk...

Yet, in primitivist logic all of these things were reckoned dust indeed. Apostolic faith was far too spare and simple an affair to embrace such complexities, and in truth they played no discernible part in the biblical record. As Scott laid bare the original gospel, therefore, a new focus of devotion must emerge, and what better could uplift and inspire the human spirit than direct exposure to the wonders and wondrous teachings of first times? For him, at least, it was contact with biblical scenes and truths through reading, memory, and the two sacraments that became the supreme spiritual exercise and spurred flights of devotion. So, after all, if in a restricted sense, "the religion of Christ [remained]...a religion of feeling as well as of faith." As Scott himself declared in 1835, "In relation to enthusiasm, [I] plead guilty. A cold medium must be exceedingly offensive to Jesus Christ."[34]

[34]Scott, *GR*, p. 224; *The Evangelist* (1 September 1835): p. 205.

CHAPTER SIX

Bringing a Vision to Life: Walter Scott and the Restored Church

D. Newell Williams

Walter Scott, born at Moffat, Scotland, October 31, 1796, has often been identified along with Barton W. Stone and Thomas and Alexander Campbell as one of the "four founders" of the movement represented today by the Christian Church (Disciples of Christ), the Churches of Christ, and the Christian Churches and Churches of Christ.[1] Known by a variety

[1]The first published identification of Stone, the Campbells, and Scott as the "big four" among the founders of the movement may have been Errett Gates, *The Disciples of Christ* (New York: Baker and Taylor Co., 1905), p. 141. Gates indicates that he was reporting a common view. Other early twentieth-century historians to identify Stone, the Campbells, and Scott as "the four founders" of the movement were Jesse J. Haley, *Makers and Molders of the Reformation Movement: A Study of Leading Men among the Disciples of Christ* (St. Louis: Christian Board of Publication, 1914), p. 59; and Walter Wilson Jennings, *Origin and Early History of the Disciples of Christ* (Cincinnati: Standard Publishing Co., 1919), who cites Haley. J. H. Garrison had offered a different list of four, substituting Robert Richardson for Barton W. Stone, *The Reformation of the Nineteenth Century* (St. Louis: Christian Publishing Co., 1901), p. 63. J. H. Garrison was followed by W. T. Moore, *A Comprehensive History of the Disciples of Christ* (New York: Fleming H. Revell Co., 1909). Moore included Stone in a second group of four along with John Smith, John Rogers, and John T. Johnson. W. E. Garrison and A. T. De Groot, *The Disciples of Christ: A History* (St. Louis: The Bethany Press, 1948) endorsed Gates's list of four and have been followed by later historians.

of names since the nineteenth century, this movement is increasingly referred to today as the Stone-Campbell movement. This name recognizes the prominent roles of Stone and the Campbells in the movement's early history and avoids using other names understood as implying particular interpretations of that history.[2]

Though Walter Scott's name does not appear in the increasingly popular name for the movement, Scott played a distinctive role. His ministry deserves recognition by contemporary members of the Stone-Campbell movement, especially at this time of the two hundredth anniversary of his birth. Moreover, the distinctive role Scott played in the early history of the movement is one contemporary Christians who face the challenge of increasingly unchurched communities may well want to examine.

Scott shared with the Campbells and Stone a vision of a restored church. Based upon their reading of the New Testament, these leaders described a God who was accessible to all people. They preached about the importance of understanding the church as a united community. This vision of the apostolic church stood in sharp contrast to their perception of the church of their time. Scott's biographer, William Baxter, described their experience:

> When they looked at the primitive church walking in the fear of God and the comfort of the Holy Spirit, and being greatly multiplied; and then at the differences, discourse, and divisions of those claiming to be followers of the meek and lowly One...the question would rise unbidden: Are these the fruits of the teachings of him who came to save a lost world?[3]

The answer, of course, was no. Such an answer provided them with a challenge: how would they bring their vision of the apostolic church to life in nineteenth-century America? Scott's efforts toward this end differed from those of Stone and the Campbells. The differences help to reveal the distinctive character of Scott's contribution to the movement.

---

[2]The name Disciples of Christ, sometimes used for the movement as a whole, is also used to distinguish the branch of the movement now known as the Christian Church (Disciples of Christ) from other branches of the movement. The term Restoration Movement has come to be identified with traditional Churches of Christ and Independent Christian Church interpretations of the movement.

[3]William Baxter, *Life of Elder Walter Scott: with sketches of his fellow-laborers, William Hayden, Adamson Bentley, John Henry, and Others* (Cincinnati: Bosworth, Chase & Hall, 1874), pp. 13–14.

Stone and the Campbells placed their emphasis on the reform of existing churches. In 1804, Kentucky pastor Barton Stone rejected party names and confessions of faith and called Christians to return to the fellowship and unity of the New Testament church. In 1809, Pennsylvania preacher and teacher Thomas Campbell published the *Declaration and Address* of the Christian Association of Washington County, Pennsylvania. That document issued a call to Christians to give up divisive traditions and to return to the unity of the apostolic church. In 1823, Thomas' son, western Virginia farmer and preacher Alexander Campbell, launched the *Christian Baptist* to attack evils and abuses in the existing churches and to champion the order and practices of the primitive church.

Walter Scott placed his emphasis on the conversion of persons from outside the churches. He began this distinctive effort on the Western Reserve (Northeastern Ohio) in 1827 as the evangelist of the Mahoning Baptist Association. In the words of Baxter, "Scott perceived that in addition to the evils of partyism in the church, that there was an equal defect in the presentation of the gospel to the world, to the remedy of which he addressed himself with signal ability and success." Baxter continued, "Making the apostles his model, he went before the world with the same plea, urging upon his hearers the same message, in the same order, with the same conditions and promises, and inviting instant compliance with its claims."[4] In other words, Scott applied what he and others had learned of the teaching and practice of the apostles to persons outside the church.

A striking example of Scott's application of what he perceived to be apostolic teaching and practice to the situation of the unchurched is evident in the development of his teaching on the design or purpose of baptism. Scott evidently first encountered the "germs" of the teaching on baptism that would figure so prominently in his later preaching in a pamphlet published in 1820 by a Scot's Baptist congregation in New York City. After noting several passages of the New Testament that refer to baptism, the writers of the pamphlet concluded:

> No one who has been in the habit of considering [baptism] merely as an *ordinance*, can read these passages with attention, without being surprised at the wonderful powers and qualities and effects and uses which are there

---

[4]Baxter, p. 15.

> apparently ascribed to it. If the language employed respecting it, in many of the passages, were to be taken literally, it would import, that *remission of sins* is to be obtained by baptism, that an *escape from the wrath to come* is effected in baptism; that *men are born the children of God* by baptism, that *salvation* is connected with baptism; that men *wash away their sins* by baptism; that men become *dead to sin and alive to God*, by baptism; that the Church of God is *sanctified and cleansed* by baptism; that men are *regenerated* by baptism; and that the *answer of a good conscience* is obtained by baptism.[5]

The congregation that produced the pamphlet did not see any application to the "unchurched" in its examination of the New Testament references to baptism. Rather, for the authors of the pamphlet, the significance of their study of baptism was to raise the question as to "how far any can now be known or recognized or acknowledged as Disciples, as having made the Christian profession, as having put on Christ, as having passed from death to life, who have not been baptized as the Disciples were." Applying the Scot's Baptist understanding of the New Testament teaching and practice of baptism to the unconverted, Scott came to believe that baptism offers persons who believe the gospel of God's grace in Jesus Christ, and repent of their sins, an assurance of the forgiveness of their sins and the gift of the Holy Spirit (the *experience* of God's presence in their lives).

Scott also applied other elements of what he found to be apostolic or New Testament teaching and practice to the situation of the unconverted. With Stone and the Campbells, Scott understood the New Testament to define faith as simple belief. Christian faith was simple belief in God's love for sinners made known in Jesus Christ. This idea differed significantly from the teaching about faith present in various American churches. Many Protestants described faith as an experience for which the unconverted were to pray. According to these leaders, faith resulted from an external experience brought on by the Holy Spirit. Scott, and other early Disciples leaders, understood the New Testament to say that the Holy Spirit is given not to the unconverted to make them repent and believe, as many churches taught, but to the church to enliven its communication of the gospel to the unconverted.

[5]Baxter, p. 51.

Scott also believed the New Testament declared that repentance or reformation is produced by faith in the message of God's love for sinners. Thus, repentance follows faith. This notion, once again, differed from the teaching of many churches, which advised the unconverted to seek repentance or reformation so they might experience faith.

Reflecting on these ideas, along with the Scot's Baptist view of baptism, Scott reached the conclusion that the New Testament commanded three things the unconverted must do, and even set forth a necessary sequence in which they are to be done: believe the gospel, repent or reform, and be immersed. Scott further concluded that attached to these three things are three gifts that God gives that are also sequentially related: the forgiveness of sins, the Holy Spirit (which Scott asserted would not abide in an unforgiven heart), and eternal life. For Scott, this was the gospel, with its elements in right order—the gospel restored; this was the message to be preached to the unchurched![6]

Concerned by reports of Scott's efforts on the Western Reserve, Alexander Campbell, who had nominated Scott in August of 1827 to serve as evangelist of the Mahoning Baptist Association, sent his father, Thomas Campbell, to observe Scott's ministry in the spring of 1828. After his visit with Scott, the elder Campbell filed a report that has continued to define Scott's distinctive contribution to the movement.

> I perceive that theory and practice in religion, as well as in other things, are matters of distinct consideration. It is one thing to know concerning the art of fishing—for instance, the rod, the line, the hook, and the bait, too; and quite another thing to handle them dexterously when thrown into the water, so as to make it take. We have long known the…theory…and have spoken and published many things *correctly concerning* the ancient gospel, its simplicity and perfect adaptation to the present state of mankind, for the benign and gracious purposes of his immediate relief and complete salvation; but I must confess that, in respect to

---

[6]Dwight E. Stevenson, *Walter Scott: Voice of the Golden Oracle* (St. Louis: Christian Board of Publication, 1946) chronicles the development of Scott's plan of salvation. See pp. 18–63. For a recent discussion of theological influences that shaped Scott's plan, see William A. Gerrard, *Walter Scott, American Frontier Evangelist* (College Press Publishing Co., 1992), pp. 49–86.

> the *direct exhibition* and *application* of it for that blessed purpose, I am at present for the first time upon the ground where the thing has appeared to be *practically exhibited* to the proper purpose.[7]

Scott took the message of the Stone-Campbell movement and addressed it, not to the church, but rather primarily to the world. This constituted his major contribution to the movement.

His initial ministry on the Western Reserve (a period of three years) netted over 3,000 additions to the churches of the Mahoning Baptist Association.[8] Though Scott directed his ministry to persons who today would be termed "unchurched," many of his converts were not actually strangers to the church. Often, the unchurched in frontier America, as in contemporary North America, had been exposed to the church at some point in their lives, but for various reasons they had not identified with it.

Ironically, the phenomenal growth of new members who affirmed the teachings of Scott in the churches of the Mahoning Association alarmed Baptists who opposed the movement associated with Campbell. Soon, this opposition led to the separation of the Disciples, or Reformers, from the Baptists. Scott continued to engage in evangelistic work for another thirty years after his initial foray into the Western Reserve, though often combining his evangelistic efforts in latter years with editorial tasks, a pastorate, or college presidency. Even in those years, it was not unusual for him to report one hundred conversions a month.[9]

---

[7]Baxter, pp. 158–159. Historians of the movement have generally accepted Thomas Campbell's appraisal of Scott's contribution. Accounts of Scott's ministry typically quote Campbell's letter followed by a statement such as that of Garrison and DeGroot, "It was he [Scott] who formulated and put into practice the effective evangelistic method which had been lacking..." See A. S. Hayden, *Early History of the Disciples in the Western Reserve, Ohio* (Cincinnati: Chase and Hall Publishers, 1875), p. 78; Moore, p. 190; M. M. Davis, *How the Disciples Began and Grew* (Cincinnati: The Standard Publishing Co., 1915), p. 208; Dean E. Walker, *Adventuring For Christian Unity: A Survey of the History of the Churches of Christ* (Birmingham, England: The Berean Press, 1935), p. 31; William E. Tucker and Lester McAllister, *Journey in Faith: A History of the Christian Church* (Disciples of Christ) (St. Louis: The Bethany Press, 1975), pp. 130–133. While the earlier accounts praise Scott's contribution, two more recent accounts also argue that Scott contributed to a "hardening" or radicalizing of Alexander Campbell's teaching on baptism. See Henry E. Webb, *In Search of Christian Unity: A History of the Restoration Movement* (Cincinnati: Standard Publishing, 1990), pp. 137–138, and Richard T. Hughes, *Reviving the Ancient Faith: The Story of Churches of Christ in America* (Grand Rapids: William B. Eerdmans Publishing Co., 1996), pp. 48–54.

[8]Gerrard, p. 35.

[9]Baxter, p. 332.

Christians today, facing the challenge of increasingly unchurched communities, might well ask, How did he do it? Scott's evangelistic ministry had at least six distinctive characteristics.

First, Scott went to the unconverted. To be sure, ministers in other churches, in particular the Methodists, did the same. However, Scott's example was a first for the Baptist churches identified with the reforming efforts of Thomas and Alexander Campbell. The hallmark of Scott's ministry involved his preaching, not to the church, but to whomever would listen. The setting of his ministry was sometimes a church or meeting house, but quite often a home, a school house, or a grove; in short, wherever he could gather a group of inquirers. Scott's ministry may be, then, something of a precedent in the Stone-Campbell tradition for the current church growth teaching that services for the unchurched should be conducted in spaces where they gather for other purposes.

Second, he was not adverse to unconventional means of advertising his efforts. The story has often been told of how one day, while riding into a village, he came upon a group of children returning home from school. He asked the children to hold up their left hands; then, beginning with their thumbs, and pointing to one finger after another, he had them repeat "faith," "repentance," "baptism," "remission of sins," "gift of the Holy Spirit." He then instructed the children to tell their parents that a man would be preaching at the schoolhouse that night on their fingers! When evening came, a waiting audience packed the schoolhouse.[10]

Another story, often told, involves an occasion when Scott found himself faced with a small congregation, made up primarily of children. Rather than preach, he told a few humorous stories and announced a meeting for the following night. When a companion asked him about this procedure, he explained the stories were bait and that they would have a large crowd the following night. When the next evening arrived, Scott and his companion had to press their way through a thick crowd to the pulpit.[11]

Third, Scott understood that the subject of Christian preaching is Jesus Christ, and him crucified. On this "fact" to be believed hinged both the commands and the promises of the Christian life. In the latter part of his ministry he commented critically on the sermons he heard, asking, "How is it that so many are blind to the greatest truths in our religion—that Messiah is God's Son? How is

[10]Stevenson, p. 74.
[11]Ibid., pp. 86–87.

it that Mount Calvary, and the death scene there, are so frequently evaded?"[12] He described two sermons he had heard recently. One was "a composition, distinguished for grace and literary finish, on the art of raising money!" Another was "Fire and brimstone—a browbeating of the audience, utterly unalleviated by the introduction of any part of the structure of the gospel."[13]

Earlier he had advised young evangelists on the content of preaching, urging that the first task is to present "in the boldest possible relief" the divine revelation that Jesus is the Son of God, not "to prove the truth" of the revelation, but to show that it is "fundamental, and the thing to be believed and confessed..."[14] As Scott stated the matter in 1836, "That God so loved the world as to give his only begotten Son, that whosoever believeth in him might not perish but have everlasting life, is of a most powerful nature to reform and purify mankind."[15]

Fourth, Scott recognized that effective preaching witnesses to the power of the Holy Spirit. On more than one occasion, he began his sermon by asking his hearers to pray to God that the Spirit might empower his efforts. The following is an example:

> Brethren and fellow-citizens: In all cases of public speaking, in the forum, at the bar, or in the pulpit, what is attempted should be done with power. Weakness is nearly allied to failure which admits not of apology, for audiences do not assemble to be tortured, wearied, disappointed, but instructed, persuaded, delighted. You are present this evening to hear of Jesus and the great redemption, and I to address you on these solemn and delightful themes. Tremblingly alive to the responsibilities of the occasion, I may be pardoned if, in view of them, I exclaim with the holy apostle, "Who is sufficient to these things?" David

[12]Quoted in Baxter, p. 327.

[13]Ibid., pp. 328–329.

[14]Quoted in Baxter, p. 332. The second task of preaching for Scott was to "prove" the truth of the revelation. What is accepted as truth is socially and historically conditioned; thus, an argument that is convincing in one time and place may not be as convincing in another. In short, Scott's sermons would need to be updated for many of the unchurched in contemporary North America! But the bottom line for Scott remains the same: The "proposition" that Jesus is the Christ is the truth on which the whole of the gospel hangs. Thus, for Scott, the proclamation of that proposition was the fundamental task of Christian preaching.

[15]Walter Scott, *The Gospel Restored* (Cincinnati: Ormsby H. Donagh, 1836), p. 188.

says, "When I called upon thee, thou answeredst me, and strengthenedst me with strength in my soul." If distrust in my own powers impels me to place a higher reliance on God, my humility shall not hurt me. Pray for me, then, dear audience, that he who faints not, neither is weary, may strengthen me with all might by his Spirit in the inner man; that I may, with all saints, comprehend the heights and depths, and length and breadth, and know the love of Christ that passeth knowledge; that I may be filled with all the fullness of God; that I may open my mouth as I ought; and to him be eternal praises.[16]

Scott's preaching of Jesus Christ with the authority, or power, of the Holy Spirit could move even the usually reserved Alexander Campbell to praise God aloud! R. R. Sloan reported the event.

Walter Scott, about 1829 or 1830, paid a visit to western Virginia, and on one occasion preached in the woods between Wellsburg and Wheeling; the audience was large, the preacher more than usually animated by his theme; near him sat Alexander Campbell, usually calm and self-contained, but in this case more fully under the influence of the preacher's eloquence than he had ever been of mortal man before; his eyes flashed and his face glowed as he heard him unfold the glories of redemption, the dignity and compassion of its author, and the honors that awaited those who would submit to his reign, until so filled with rapture and an admiration, not of the speaker, but of him who was his theme, that he cried out, "Glory to God in the highest," as the only way to relieve the intensity of his joy.[17]

Scott's nineteenth century biographer, noting that Mr. Campbell was naturally not very demonstrative, added "this was perhaps the only case in which his feelings so completely carried him away."[18]

Fifth, Scott recognized the power of the arts in human communication. The son of a music teacher, Scott had a pleasant singing voice and also played the flute. Early in his ministry as

---

[16]Quoted in Baxter, p. 324.
[17]Quoted in Baxter, p. 220.
[18]Baxter, pp. 220–221.

evangelist of the Mahoning Association, Scott chose a younger preacher, William Hayden as his fellow laborer or assistant. Asked to explain his choice, Scott pointed to Hayden's musical abilities, remarking, "There is not a man in the Association that can sing like him."[19] Baxter wrote of Hayden, "He had a voice of great depth and compass, at one time sweet and melodious as the south wind's sigh, at another, swelling out into tempest tones." He added, "He instructed his hearers by his speech, but he melted and moved them by his songs, and all who knew him remembered him as the sweet singer."[20]

Scott's appreciation for the role of music in communicating the full meaning of the Christian gospel was reflected in his editing of hymnbooks and his conducting of schools to teach young people the musical skills necessary to sing hymns. "It is the office of a hymn," Scott wrote, "to arouse impassioned devotional feeling, even as it is the office of teaching to illuminate understanding."[21] Noting that both Alexander Campbell and Stone wrote hymns of disputed quality, Peter Morgan has observed that Scott's respect for high musical standards may explain why he, in contrast to the Campbells and Stone composed no known tunes and wrote no known hymn texts![22]

Of course, Scott's oratory was art. Notice the poetic quality of his description of the power of God made known in the gospels: "In the evangelists we behold the everlasting, the unexpended power itself, revealed in the form of a servant, and with more than a servant's humility, the strength of the Lion of the tribe of Judah, and harmlessness of the Lamb dwelling together in the same one." Imagine the following text delivered in the Scottish brogue he never lost:

> Methinks I see the cross thrown down upon the ground, and the great substitute for man racked to the dimensions of its cursed limbs! Exhausted and forlorn, the hands that aye were filled with blessings and deeds of love and charity, are rudely seized by the iron handed Roman, and nailed to the murderous wood; the feet, those feet that ever trod the path of peace, are spiked and barred to make the offering sure! Death! Death! Horrible in every shape! But in

---

[19]Ibid, p. 200.

[20]Ibid.

[21]Peter Morgan, "Disciples Hymnbooks: A continuing Quest for Harmony," *Discipliana* 55:2 (Summer 1995), p. 50.

[22]Ibid., pp. 47–51.

> this, clothing the terror with pains tenfold more terrible than flesh and blood dare encounter. Good God, 'tis violence all to crucify a man; and murder infinite to crucify the Son; for who has lived to tell the pain extreme he felt, when all his sacred person came down upon the nails and spikes that pierced him?[23]

Sixth, though never an extemporaneous preacher, Scott attended to his audience, and could respond to particular circumstances. Once, when preaching on the atonement, Scott noticed his audience going to sleep. He abruptly addressed himself to the young boys on the front row. Discovering they were familiar with a game called "toad sky-high" (a game in which one leans a plank on a stone, places a toad on the lower end of the plank, then pounds the elevated end of the plank with a stick), he proceeded happily to tell the children about playing this game as a boy in Scotland. The boys laughed. Changing his demeanor, Scott informed the boys that toad sky-high was really a bad game, since the toad often died. He continued with a description of a toad's death so vivid that some to the boys began to cry. Turning to their parents he declared, "Your children are weeping over the death of a toad, while you have been sleeping though the story of the death of your Lord!"[24]

Does Scott's example have anything to teach contemporary North American Christians? Surely it does. It teaches us to go to the unchurched, to let the public know what it is we do, to preach Jesus Christ, to remember that effective preaching witnesses to the power of the Holy Spirit, to use the arts, to be flexible. Scott's example also teaches us to have a vision and, more importantly, what that vision should be. Though we may use different language, we will not improve much on his vision of a restored church—a church possessing the gospel of Jesus Christ as the foundation upon which the unity that Christ gives is maintained and grows. To bring that vision to life among both the churched and unchurched living in the late twentieth century is a great challenge facing the contemporary church.

---

[23]Scott, pp. 404–405. Hayden, p. 94, refers to "the brogue of his native Scotch tongue."

[24]Stevenson, pp. 75–76.

CHAPTER SEVEN

Shall We Preach the "R" Word Again?

Fred B. Craddock

Well, my task is rather simple. I want to enlist your help in the rehabilitation of a word, and I do so assuming an audience friendly to that task, given your own excellent record of preserving and caring for the vocabulary of the church. That is a part of our assignment as Christians and as Christian leaders. It involves a lot of things, sometimes. It involves recovering words that are stolen, as many of us did a few years ago when the word "charisma" was stolen. Somebody broke into the church and took it; we discovered it especially among the entertainers and the politicians, but we were able to recover it and, in some churches, put it back in the vault.

Sometimes our work involves trying to restore the respect that is due a word, like the word "charity." I was a character witness for charity in the Superior Court of DeKalb County in Georgia a few years ago. The charge against charity was that she was loitering, guilty of vagrancy, being seen often on the dirty streets where the poverty and crime is heavy in southwest Atlanta. She had been seen around Goodwill stores and Salvation Army posts and soup kitchens. I told the judge that is where she belonged. Well, if she is so good, why isn't she up on the northern side of town, where the nice people live? And she was sentenced to a hundred hours of community service, and when she received the sentence she laughed because she knew that's what she'd be doing anyway.

Sometimes this care for the church's vocabulary means putting some words into retirement. They've become quaint, out of place, misunderstood, no longer used. I enjoy attending these retirement services. We had a nice one in Louisville, about four years ago—a lot of speakers at the retirement of "right smart." Many folk have felt that it was no longer in use. I still got right smart good out of it, but it was retired.

In Kansas City, "meet" was retired—m, double e, t. I was sad about that. It has such an excellent history coming from the Saxon into the Anglo. Not everybody agreed. There was a little circle of protesters with signs outside the building, a delegation from one of the local Episcopal churches, and I asked them, "Oh, why are you out here with these signs protesting?" And they said, "It is meet and right, so to do." So I guess the word isn't dead.

Some of you may have noticed in the paper, if you live in the Southwest, the postponement of the retirement service over in Dallas. It was to be a retirement for the word "gumption." There was a lot of ugly opposition to it. I got a nasty note myself, saying, "You have some gumption, trying to retire this word."

I have a word in mind that I'd like for you to help me rehabilitate. It hasn't become quaint; it has not fallen into silence. It has become soiled through distortion, exaggeration, cartooning, and laughter. I have in mind the word "repentance." Shall we preach repentance again? I shudder to think of the loss to the church, and the loss to all of the people to whom we will preach and do preach, if we lose that word. Now, it's not going to be easy, this rehabilitation. It's going to be very difficult, because repentance has enemies, ancient and modern.

Aristotle, for instance, said that repentance is a flaw of character. It shows a lack of consistency and character if someone repents. The rabbis of centuries ago had difficulty with this and especially with the people who presumed upon repentance. There were some who thought you could repent in advance. If you were planning a little hokeypokey, you could go ahead and repent and have that out of the way, and then you would enjoy what you were going to do. The rabbis warned against this effort to repent ahead of time. Repentance suffered somewhat, though it was given some place in the culture by being calendarized. There are days of repentance, ritualized with sack cloth and ashes. And the church followed suit. We have days of repentance. Just a touch of it at Advent, and a heavy dose during Lent. With the ashes there are times to repent, and times not to think about it.

The word has been novelized since the days of Augustine. All western biography and autobiography has been written according to the framework of the centrality of repentance, though often the word is never used. But the format of all novels, of a biographical or autobiographical nature, has been the same. My life was this way, there was a radical turn, and now my life is this way. Call the radical turn what you will. But it is embedded in repentance and in that novelizing of our world.

It has been resisted by people who feel they are victims. Our fathers and mothers ate the sour grapes. Why should we repent? It has also been cartooned. Some sweaty evangelist under a tent in a wheat field in Kansas, mustering up a lot of manufactured indignation like a noisy squirrel, calling everybody to repentance, and we laugh. How 1920-ish that is. And yet, lose this word and we have lost more than we know.

You know as well as I, how important it is in the New Testament—not evenly so among all the writers. I'm surprised myself that, though the thought is there, the vocabulary of repentance is rather scarce in the writings of Paul. I'm sure you've noticed. But not in Revelation, and certainly not in that literary figure who wrote those two marvelous volumes, the person we call Luke, almost going out of his way to put the word in there. And if Mark tells a story and the word isn't there, Luke tells the story again and puts the word in there. Listen to Mark: "Jesus said, 'I have not come to call the righteous, but sinners.'" Listen to Luke: "Jesus said, 'I have not come to call the righteous, but sinners to repentance. Unless you repent, you shall all likewise perish.'"

Just at the time of his departure, according to Luke 24, Jesus announced that repentance and forgiveness of sin were to be preached to all nations. That, for Luke, is the gospel: repentance and forgiveness of sin, and so the second volume begins, "Repent and be baptized everyone of you. Repent and turn again, that seasons of refreshing will come from the presence of God." The times of ignorance, God has overlooked. For now God commands that everyone repent. And in that most beautiful of all the expressions, found in Acts 11, when Simon Peter is reporting back to Jerusalem after his experience in the house of Cornelius in Caesaria, Simon Peter said to the church in Jerusalem, "God has granted the gift of repentance to all people."

Hear that? "The gift of repentance to all people." And the marvelous thing about our tradition is that the word was recovered, and understood, by our forebears in this tradition. I think they tried to make too fine a point out of the two different words in the Greek text for repentance, calling one remorse and the other reform, and using Judas as an example of remorse, who, caught up in his own self-pity, took his own life. Simon Peter, who turned about and was useful to Christ, is used as the example of reforming. Those two words, I think, cannot be found just exactly that way everywhere they occur. But even so, they were studious in the matter of recovering the meaning of this word. To reform. And they preached it.

I thought I would appeal to you for your help in this matter, on behalf of the memory of Walter Scott, a marvelous man, with such a large interior world. If he were living today, somebody would probably say, correctly or not, that he was manic depressive. He could soar, and he could sink. Such a large world inside himself. He took the pain of a divided church personally. And when the Civil War began, he took the pain of a divided nation personally. Sometimes unable to eat. Sometimes refusing to share fully in the worship service. Eating away at his soul was all this sin. This remarkable man who died and lay for thirty-seven years in an unmarked grave, over whose casket a sermon was preached at his funeral with that melancholy text, Isaiah 57:1. "The righteous perish, and no one takes it to heart."

I thought I would appeal to you by his memory, this man who gave us what I think is the propositional equivalent of a governing metaphor. The propositional equivalent of a governing narrative, whereby we might read the text of scripture. It was simple, it was clear, it was portable—faith, repentance, baptism, forgiveness of sin, gift of the Holy Spirit. This man, who understood repentance not as just a feeling, not standing paralyzed in a pool of pity, but reformation of life—mind and body and will—and demonstrating such by acts of charity, benevolence, generosity, honesty, and dependability.

I thought I could make a case with you by drawing upon your fond memory of him, but I changed my mind. Decided not to do that. I decided to back away and appeal to you on what may be a deeper, more lasting, and perhaps more honest basis. And that is, I appeal to you to preach the "R" word again, on the behalf of all the men and women and young people who are going to hear us preach. All of those people who, lacking the opportunity by a simple urging to repentance, lacking the opportunity to feel again the fresh visitations of the Spirit of God, just a simple appeal to drop the baggage. Make only healthy relationships. Give your life to the needs of other people. Drop and lose all grudges that you don't want anyway. Let your life be trim and chaste and clean and clear and free before God. Can we not say that without appearing to be sweaty evangelists? If you don't, if you don't, you will deny a lot of people the opportunity to feel what in the history of the church has been called the scattering of the clouds. What others have called the lifting of burdens. What the scripture calls a new beginning, a new birth, a new creation. I urge you to make this appeal.

Now, if you do, it means that you're going to have to move past the appearances and the self-deception and the disguises that people wear, people appearing to be very secular and uninterested in all of this. Don't let that fool you. I used to think hypocrisy was pretending to be religious when you weren't. The modern form of hypocrisy is pretending to be secular when you're not. We have to move past that, to speak to what is really there, even not clearly known to the person to whom you speak, because some have been derailed into a kind of pop righteousness. They put a bumper sticker on, "Save the Spotted Owl," and think they've done their duty for Jesus and then stand in those screaming lines for five hours to get the autograph of some drugged-up, drunk-up movie star or sport star. To cry two hours through a movie about the sad fate of children and leave the theater and step over the homeless on the way to the car. "Save the Spotted Owl." You're not fooling anybody.

On the other hand, those who are into that pop morality, taking a stand, produce many forms of cruelty to which are attached the name of Jesus. These are people who, if the prodigal comes home, would arrest him. Six years for you mandated. I have been hearing such cruelty with the name of Jesus attached. It happened in Georgia, at the prison where the executions take place. A crowd of people outside with banners. Here's this big poster. I saw it on television. It had Jesus' name. There was another one, had a verse of scripture on it. The warden came out and said, "At exactly 12:09 this person was pronounced dead." Yes, praise the Lord.

Human beings! Taking a stand. It'll be hard for you to get through that, to the real need, but we must. We must not be fazed nor fooled nor seduced by those who have an apparent good life, wonderful life. Things are going well. They have a fist full of twenty dollar bills, but they have never yet found the market where life is sold. And when they die, what happens to all that? It will be piled in the yard, and an auctioneer will gavel it away to strangers who are crawling over their personal effects.

Is that it? Bedazzled by the pictures in the paper of this beautiful young woman, a debutante, coming out in society, making her way down the winding stairs to a adoring crowd below, as she enters society. And yet, off in the country in a cabin doorway, a fifteen-year-old girl with a young 'un on her hip, stares off into a world that holds no hope. She has one thing. She has a red dress in the closet. And Monday she'll leave the baby with a neighbor, and she'll put on that red dress and take her love to town. And then we'll scream, "Ah, what's happening to the young people today!" We can't be fooled by all that difference. It is not that different. We must be able to look and listen beyond what people want, to what they need, and that is extremely, extremely difficult.

I recommend to you a book by Lucy Grealy, *The Autobiography of a Face*. Whenever you are finished with Thomas Aquinas, you might pick it up. It's a little book. It's, as she says, an autobiography. She's a young woman when she writes it. When she was a teenager it was discovered she had a malignancy in the jaw, both in the bone and in the flesh. It was cut out. She had the treatments, the burning treatments. More cutting, more treatments. Some of the surgery was to repair her face. Some of the surgery was to take away her face. Over thirty surgeries. Building, cutting away, building, cutting away. In the meantime, she pulled the blinds; she stayed at home. She let her hair grow long and let it hang over that side of her face. She bought floppy hats and wore them down on that side of her face. And she thought, in bitterness and anger and envy and jealousy: If I only had a new face, if I only had a new face, if I only had a new face; she said, "It took me fifteen years to face the real question—if I only had a new heart." Not bitter, not envious, not cold, not angry. Fifteen years, she said.

We have an immense ability at self-deception. When I was pastoring a little church in Tennessee, I thought I would meet the needs of the people and put the grease where the squeak was. So I said, "I'm putting up a question box out in the foyer, and any question you have, you want to ask, just write it down. Put it in the box. Indicate if you think it's something to be preached from the pulpit, to be dealt with in Sunday school, or to talk about in private;

just indicate your preference." It was a technique of what I would think of today as a sort of consumer-driven church.

I got a lot of questions. I left the thing up two weeks. Took it down. Biggest mistake of my life. "Where did Cain get his wife?" "Did the waters of the flood cover the whole earth or just the Near East?" "Do you think the earth is millions of years old or was Bishop Ussher right in dating the creation?" "Do you think it was six days like we have today?" "Can you identify the antichrist?" "What does it mean, 666, in Revelation?" "Are we experiencing the times, the last times, spoken of in the Apocalypse?" On and on they went. Who asked me these questions? Who asked me these questions? There were people whose daughters were pregnant well before marriage, whose sons were alcoholic before they left high school. People who, themselves, were as greedy as goats. People who were caught up in upward mobility and the spiral to something better, socially and economically. People who were profoundly prejudiced against anyone black or Hispanic, who would never have wanted any of them inside the church. These people asked me where Cain got his wife.

What should they have asked? Who has the nerve to really ask the question, what are we to do? Ladies and gentlemen, what are we to do? The past is irreparable. All the king's horses and all the king's men will not put my world together again. What are we to do? I'm sure some of you wonder, if I were to preach repentance how would I do it? Shall we go back to those early days, when the gospel was preached for an hour, hour-and-a-half? And when the gospel sermon, the good news of God's grace, was finished, the preacher would sit down and an exhorter would stand up, sometimes one of the elders, and then call on the people to repent and be baptized for the forgiveness of sin and the gift of the Holy Spirit.

I remind you, by the way, that that's the way it was in Acts. Simon Peter and the others, they preached the gospel. This Jesus of Nazareth, whose way of life you all know, it's public record. This Jesus of Nazareth, crucified at the hands of lawless people; you know that. You were part of it. This Jesus of Nazareth, God has raised from the dead; of that we are witnesses. Therefore, let you all know God has made him Lord in Christ, this Jesus whom you crucified, and it was when they were pricked in their hearts that they preached repentance. But how can that be achieved?

Well, it's a good question. I know we have varieties of gifts, varieties of ministries. When Paul talks about varieties of ministries and varieties of gifts, I think he's entering into the world that we would call imagination. To imagine, how can we do this? How can I do this? How can the church do this? How can this be effective again? That calls for some sort of chastened and sanctified imagination. How to do it? That's a good question.

I've been reading about the American church following the Civil War up to the present, and I think I never noticed a period, a fruitful period of time before and following 1900, when ministers spent a lot of time saying, "How are we going to reach the public? How are we going to reach the public?" And one way that was conceived, and very effective, was writing Christian novels. Christian novels. We read them now, and they're not really heavy enough for us, but they were powerful.

The three most effective, *Uncle Tom's Cabin, Ten Knights in a Barroom*, and *In His Steps*. *In His Steps*—twenty-three million copies in English alone, within the first ten years, not counting the dozens of translations in other languages from that Kansas Congregational minister who sat in prayer and thought and said, "How are we going to do it?" Do you worry about that? Do you think about that? How are we going to do it? Our ministries are so brief, the world is so large, the problems are so deep. Stir my mind and my imagination to think of a way.

I heard a reporter interviewing Charles Kuralt. It was sometime after he had retired from that "Sunday Morning" program I never got to see. It came during church, and I had to choose between Charles and Jesus, and Charles came in second. But he was being interviewed:

"What are you doing, now that you are retired?"

"I am now doing research on the Lewis and Clark Expedition. We're going to have the bicentennial in two thousand and four. The trip to the northwest was, ah, 1804, 1806. We'll be having the bicentennial soon, and I'm doing the research."

"Well, Mr. Kuralt, do you plan to write a history or biography of these two men? What do you plan to do?"

And he said, "No, no, no, no. I want to get someone capable to help me and take my research and put it into a poem that children can memorize."

"Really?"

"Yeah, yeah, yeah. If we can get the school children to memorize it, it will pass into the consciousness of the American people."

Whew! Have I spent that much time really thinking about, how can we get this into the consciousness of the American people? Good question. May I say to you that it doesn't call for your putting on a lot of trappings of judgmental spirit, furrowing the brow and reminding them of the bleached bones that wash ashore from the lake of fire and all that. Judgment is in there. It was in the preaching of our forebears, and it's in the New Testament, but it's interesting that it's not *the* governing consideration. Søren Kierkergaard said one time, "Some things are true when whispered, but they become false when shouted." You write judgment in the right size print, it's right in biblical and truth. But make the print too large, it's false.

You don't have to do that. You don't *have* to actually become confrontational, just bending everybody's axle and hammering away. Not necessary. Aristotle said one time, "When it comes to the matter of catharsis, cleansing, there has to be preceding it a kind of lingering." Isn't that pretty? "Lingering." Just easing into a matter. Not throwing people into a defensive posture, with all of that, "I challenge you today." Just ease into it. That's the way good writers do.

I've been heavily influenced by the novels of Thomas Hardy. I think I'm the only one in Georgia that reads them. Maybe Texas, too. He takes so long to get started. Up on the hillside, at about page 53, when they top the hill, they look down and they see the village of Casterbridge. And the county fair is going on. Why didn't he say that on page one and let's get this thing going. It's my way of knowing I'm in the hands of someone who knows where he's going. This is going to be very, very important. Even the New Testament, with all of its brevity—it's such a little book, but every once in a while enjoys the luxury of a little lingering. There is, in Jerusalem, by the sheepgate, a pool, called in Hebrew, "Bethzatha." It has five porticos, and in these lay a multitude of sick and paralyzed and diseased. There was one man who had been there for thirty-eight years. And Jesus approached him. Ha! Isn't that great?

You remember how Pinnochio starts? Haven't read Pinnochio today? Once upon a time there was a king, my young readers will shout. No, no, my children, you're wrong. Once upon a time there was a piece of wood. Ah! That can do it. You can even, I believe this, you can even affect repentance by teaching the Bible.

Now I say this for this reason. One is, many people in our churches today do not know the Bible and, therefore, it robs you of one of the most powerful and effective ways of preaching, and that is making allusion to biblical accounts. But you can't make allusion to them if they don't know them. This was part of the power of Walter Scott's preaching, that he could assume his listeners knew the Bible, and with a wave of the hand he could allude to some story, Old or New Testament, and they knew. That's it. That's it. That's it. And there's nothing so powerful as a wakening recognition, yes. But how rare it is. How rare it is.

Fellow came to trim the tree, so dangerous and close to our back window. We hated to lose it, a big hemlock, but it had to go. It was a threat. We called this fellow, Mike Chandler. Mike looked at it, and said, "I can take it down piece by piece, won't harm the house," and so he did. But he seemed to be more than a trimmer of trees. I said to him when I paid him, I said, "Well, Mike, have you decided that this is your life?" And he said, "Interesting that you would ask. I put out my fleece on the ground just this morning. Sorry to bother you with that scripture." And I said, "And so?" And he grinned and said, "I'll put out my fleece again tomorrow."

But, boy, Walter Scott, in his sermons, those allusions, much more powerful in preaching than direct citation, is the allusion, because people lean forward and say, "Yes, that's in our Bible at home. That's our stuff you're preaching." And that is powerful, but you have to teach it first. Otherwise…

I was reading about all the cheating in schools, high schools and colleges and universities, just cheating all over the country. Even in our military academies. Catching the students cheating! So I asked around in Atlanta among some of the pastors. I said, "Do you have this problem in church, people cheating in Sunday school?" And, all of them agreed, "No, we don't have any cheating in our church." I said, "Why?" thinking perhaps they would say, "Well, after all, this is a Christian institution." But do you know what they said? How can you cheat? There is no requirement that they be there. Even the teacher doesn't show up a lot of the time. There is no assignment. There is no passing. There is no failing. There is no preparation, no expectation. How could anyone cheat?

True, but you can affect repentance by the teaching of scripture if you trust that the word will do the work. Let the house of Israel know assuredly, and like the Ethiopian eunuch, people in your presence will draw that chariot to a stop and say, "What hinders my being baptized?" when all Phillip was doing was teaching about the prophecies and Jesus.

Ah, you can do it. You can do it if your sermons just have enough size—that you set the lives of the people in the larger context of God's purpose, what we call today the metanarrative, the narrative above all other narratives, what God is doing in the world anchored before time, continuing beyond time. What a marvelous thing, especially for people in little communities and little churches, to have their lives set in something so big. It's humbling, it's turning, it's churning, and it calls forth repentance.

Did you read Umberto Eco's Norton Lectures called "Six Walks in the Woods?" You ought to read it. He said he was once invited to go to a planetarium. He loved the planetarium. And when he arrived, the time came to turn off the lights so that they could see the beauty of the simulated sky with the stars and suns and moons and all. He didn't know that the director of the planetarium knew he was coming, and so by means of the computer set the sky at a certain position—the sky as it appeared over Alessandria, Italy. "That's where I was born," said Umberto. The sky as it was on the night of January 6, 1932. "That's the night I was born," he said. "And so the sky appeared as it was in the place and the hour of my birth," and that great man said, "I was stilled, I was afraid, I was filled with a sense of peace. I could have died and it would have been all right." By what? By the very same thing you can do if you just set the lines in the metanarrative from God back to God. But if that is too much, then simply recount the goodnesses of God. That's what Paul said, you know. It's the goodness of God that leads you to repentance and it does.

In Atlanta I have been a part now, these three years, of a Sacred Harp Advent Service. Shaped notes, we have a song leader, we have a group of singers, and we have a bluegrass band called the Handsaw Brothers, and I do the speaking between the songs. It's an Advent service, and you know what Advent is. Anticipating, announcing, hoping, "Oh come, oh come, Emmanuel," and the joy that fills the room as you think of what God is doing in Jesus Christ. The place was full. We didn't have enough room. We did it a second night. It was still full.

The first night a woman came in a bit late with three children, noisy children, misbehaving children. There was no place. She made her way up noisily near the front. The children misbehaved badly all through the whole thing. The next night they were not there, but in the coffee and conversation time afterward this woman came up to me and said, "You may not recognize me, but I was the one with the three noisy children." I said, "I remember the three noisy children. How are you?" And she said, "I've come back tonight." And I said, "Well, good that you appreciated enough to come a second night." And she looked at me soberly and said, "I didn't bring the children. Why? When I go to something that I think is going to kind of get to me, I take those kids, and it keeps me distracted. And whatever is being said or sung doesn't get to me. I came back tonight without the children." And I said, "What are you saying to me?" And she said, "I have made such a mess. My life is nothing." In other words, as Luke would say, "Brothers, what are we to do?"

Those of you who preach, those of you who preach, what would you say to her? Surely, surely you could say something to her.

INDEX